# CAPTAIN JEFF

——O R——

# Frontier Life in Texas

——WITH THE——

## TEXAS RANGERS

Some Unwritten History and Facts in the Thrilling Experiences of Frontier Life. — The Battle and Death of Big Foot, the Noted Kiowa Chief.—The Mortally Wounding and Dying Confession of "Old Jape," the Comanchie, the Most Noted and Bloodthirsty Savages that Ever Depredated on the Frontier of Texas.

By One of the Nine
A Member of Company "E"
Texas Rangers.

JANAWAY PUBLISHING, INC.
Santa Maria, California

# Notice

In many older books, foxing (or discoloration) occurs and, in some instances, print lightens with wear and age. Reprinted books, such as this, often duplicate these flaws, notwithstanding efforts to reduce or eliminate them. The pages of this reprint have been digitally enhanced and, where possible, the flaws eliminated in order to provide clarity of content and a pleasant reading experience.

Copyright © 1906, W. J. Maltby

Originally Published:
Colorado, Texas
1906

Reprinted by:

Janaway Publishing, Inc.
732 Kelsey Ct.
Santa Maria, California 93454
(805) 925-1038
www.janawaygenealogy.com

2012

ISBN: 978-1-59641-268-2

*Made in the United States of America*

CAPT. W. J. MALTBY (CAPT. JEFF).
Who Killed "Big Foot," the Notorious Kiowa Chief
After Being Nine Years on His Trail.

# PREFACE.

As this narrative records the killing of two "Big Foot" Indians it is due to the reader that I give dates of killings, and the sections of country where their depredations took place.

"Big Foot" first mentioned operated west of San Antonion, over the counties of Bexar, Medina, Frio, Uvalde, Nueces, and elsewhere, and was killed by Captain William (Big Foot) Wallace in 1853. His tribe is unknown.

Big Foot No. 2 was killed by Captain W. J. Maltby, known as Captain Jeff, Commander of Company E, Frontier Battalion Texas Rangers, in the year of 1874. Big Foot No. 2 depredated over the counties of Callahan, Coleman, Brown, Llano, Mason, Burnett, Lampasas and Hamilton. His Lieutenant, Jape, or Japy, the Comanche, was mortally wounded when Big Foot was killed, and in his (Jape's) dying confession, said that Big Foot No. 2 was a Kiowa Chief, big and brave, and had just come from the Fort Sill (U. S.) Reservation.

# Publisher's Notice.

This book is written by Capt. W. J. Maltby, a noted Pioneer, Frontiersman and Texas Ranger, who did more service on the Frontier of Texas than any living man; commanding Texas Rangers nine years, and finally destroying the worst band of Indians that ever depredated on the frontier of Texas.

The story is one continued thrilling incident after another from start to finish, which holds the attention of lovers of fiction, romance and facts, and verifies the statement that facts are stranger than fiction, when told in the style of the author, with his ready wit and great store of humor.

This book pays a just and noble tribute to all who took part in the frontier life of Texas, that laid the foundation of the Empire State of the Union, The book was born of necessity and pre-eminence as a reminder to the young as well as the middle aged and the old heroes of that historical time, whne the peace and safety of Texas' future hung equally poised in the balances.

All should read "Captain Jeff," because it gives facts as they occurred and a truthful statement found in no other history or writings, and all the tediousness has been eliminated and the story told in a brief, simple and convincing manner, which makes it a book of value to all.

This book will be of inestimable value to every citizen

of Texas, or anywhere else that wants to know anything of Texas and her struggles with the redman for supremacy.

The first edition was quickly exhausted, and no doubt this second edition will be sold as rapidly.

The price in paper binding is 50 cents and in cloth $1.00 15 cents extra on each copy when sent by mail. The book can be obtained of N. C. Bawcom, Sweetwater, Texas; or Capt. W. J. Maltby, Admiral, Callahan County, Texas.

Respectfully,
N. C. BAWCOM,
Agent and Manager,
Sweetwater, Texas.

# INDEX.

**CHAPTER I.** - - - - - - - 17
    Capt. Jeff Resigned his Commission as Captain of Co. G, Seventeenth Texas Volunteer Infantry, McCullough's Brigade, Walker's Division, Feb. 19, 1863, on account of bad health, and went to his home in Burnett Co., Texas.

**CHAPTER II.** - - - - - - - 23
    Indian depredations come thick and fast and the Big Foot Indian Kiowa Chief, the most formidable enemy of the frontier, and his wonderful seeming providential escapes.

**CHAPTER III.** - - - - - - - 36
    The disobedience of orders and the timidity of the women, doubtless prolonged the wily Chief's existence.

**CHAPTER IV.** - - - - - - - 48
    The Civil War has ended. Gen. Lee has surrendered and our Captain Jeff is hounded as a wolf by Federal soldiers, in which the heroism of a true woman and noble wife is illustrated.

**CHAPTER V.** - - - - - - 55
    Captain Jeff surrenders to the Federal authorities, in which the old adags proves true a "Friend in need is a friend Indeed"

**CHAPTER VI.** - - - - - - 60
    Capt. Jeff wrongfully indited by the civil law, for which he makes a bad break, but through the Christianizing influence of the noble wife, he guards himself against like occurrences.

**CHAPTER VII.** - - - - - - 62
    His wife's little tea party.

**CHAPTER VIII.** - - - - - 65
    Richard Coke is elected governor. A battalion of Rangers is ordered. Capt. Jeff is commissioned and raises a Company, goes on duty and renews his pursuit of the Big Foot Indian.

**CHAPTER IX.** - - - - - 73
    Sergeant Andrew Mather is sent on a scout in Callahan county Camps near Caddo Peak. John Parsons is sent out to kill a deer for meat, encounters Big Foot and band, makes his celebrated shot, Big Foot dodges the bullet and makes his escape.

CHAPTER X. - - - - - - 77
    Lieutenent Best is sent on a scout. Camps on Jim Ned and is attacked after night by Big Foot and band. Cool bravery and discipline whipped him off with the loss of only one horse.

CHAPTER XI. - - - - - 80
    High water discipline and the Ranger feast.

CHAPTER XII - - - - - 85
    Sargeant Mather is sent on a scout in Runnels county in which discipline, coupled with individual bravery, kills the largest bear in West Texas with a bowie knife.

CHAPTER XIII. - - - - - 92
    Captain Jeff's lucky No. "9" and the promptings of the Still small voice fully verified.

CHAPTER XIV. - - - - - 102
    The buffalo hunt. Discipline and a lesson taught that military organization could profit by its example.

CHAPTER XV. - - - - - 107
    The reduction and discharge of the Companies and fifty men from each company in the Frontier Battalion and the return home to its peaceful pursuits.

CHAPTER XVI. - - - - 109
    Retrospective View.

CHAPTER XVII. - - - - - 111
    Finale. At Mountain Dale, Home of Captain Jeff.

Captain Maltby Honored - - - - 115

## PART II

Capt. Maltby's Reminiscences - - - - - 118
A Letter from Captain Maltby - - - - - 148

## PART III

Newspaper Extracts - - - - - - - 159
Capt. Maltby Interviewed by a Reporter - - - 172
Homes for the People, Wealth for the State and Justice for the Howlers - - - - - - - 175
Homes for the People and Wealth for the State - - 179
Capt. Maltby's letter to the Belle Plains Alliance - 182
Old Time Memories - - - - - - - 186
Fruit and Truck Growing in West Texas - - - 189
Speech by Capt. Maltby at the Illinois State Fair - 193
They were Comanches and Kiowas - - - - 201

# CAPTAIN JEFF

## CHAPTER I.

Capt. Jeff Resigned his Commission as Captain of Co. G, Seventeenth Tex. Volunteer Infantry, McCullough's Brigade, Walker's Division, Feb. 19, 1863, on account of bad health, and went to his home in Burnett Co. Texas.

On February 19th, 1863, two horsemen were seen winding their way carefully through a creek bottom that was completely covered with water for a distance of one and a half miles in width, and ever and anon a plunge into swimming water would be taken as they came to the depressions, or the sloughs, that ran through the bottom; this was on the road that leads from Pine Bluff, Ark., to Austin, Texas. Gen. John B. Walker's Division of Confederate Soldiers had gone in to winter quarters near Pine Bluff. The appearance of these horsemen denoted that they were Confederate officers or soldiers. Let us follow them to where they put up that night, and inquire who they are and where they are going.

They put up that night at Farmer Jack McClure's, seventeen miles from Gen. Walker's camp. On making the inquiry we find that one of them is Captain Jeff, who had been in command of Company "E," Seventeenth Texas Volunteer Infantry, commanded by R. T. P. Allen; G. W. Jones, Lieut. Col. The other man is Lieut. D. Reed, as traveling companion.

On making further inquiry we find that on February 18th, the day before this story commences, that Captain Jeff was regimental officer of the day, and on being relieved from duty that evening he went to Dr. Deport Smith's tent—Dr. Smith was the head of the medical board. The doctor said to him: "Captain, if you are alive in the morning, I want you to write out your resignation and bring it to me, and I will put a certificate to it that will take you out of this service at once. There is but one thing that may prolong your life for an indefinite time, and that is the life-giving atmosphere of Western Texas;" to which the captain replied: "Well, Doctor, I have great faith and respect for you as a doctor, but I have no fears of dying, being killed or drowning. Some wise man said, 'there is a Fate that shapes our ends,' etc. and something seems to tell me that I have something to live for; it may be something very commonplace; however, I will live to perform it. It seems to be in the dim future to me, but that I will live to perform whatever it may be, I haven't the least doubt."

As this is the man we are to follow as the hero of this little book, it is due the reader to give a short description of his personal appearance. He was born in Sangamon County, Ill., December 17th, 1829; is six feet high, with breast and shoulders of a lion, and weighs when in good health, two hundred pounds; with light complexion, expressive gray blue eyes, and an unconquerable will or determination. But he is at this time a mere shadow of his former physical manhood.

The second and succeeding days of his and Lieut. Reed's travels were a repetition of the first, plunging and swimming creeks, bayous and sloughs until they crossed the Trinity River some four hundred miles from where they started, which almost demonstrates that he had something to live for, or he never could have performed this journey at this inclement season of the year on horseback, and we may say with but little, if any change of apparel. But overcoming all obstacles that lay in his path, he accomplished the distance of six hundred miles to his home in twenty-five days, where he found his true and devoted wife and two sweet children, Jeff and Mollie, in the best of health. Here, the writer's pen is inadequate to portray the happiness of that little family, so we leave the good wife and mother to fix up little dainties and nicknacks to tempt the appetite, tone up the stomach and help nature to give back life and strength to the worn and weary soldier, while little Jeff and Mollie climb on his knee, put their arms around his neck and exclaim: "My papa, my papa!" While we call on Dr. Wilson Barton, and ask him to go and lend his medical skill to make that little family completely happy, which the good doctor joyously and willingly did, and under his skillful treatment, coupled with the kind nursing of his wife and the prattle of little Jeff and Mollie, our subject soon regained his health and vigor. So on August the 9th, 1863, he donned his soldier's attire, and presented himself for duty to Col. John S. Ford, who was commander of conscripts, with headquarters at Austin, Texas.

During the years of 1862 and 1863 the Indians had become more troublesome than ever before, from its first settlement, and it was much feared that they would rob the settlers of all their work-stock until there would not be teams left to make bread for the women and children.

As Col. Ford had seen and done as much service on the frontier as any man, living or dead, and being personally acquainted with Captain Jeff, he recognized the fact at once that in the person of Captain Jeff, the opportunity was given him to do valuable service on the frontier, in the protection of life and property, so he ordered Captain Jeff to go home and to organize a company of conscripts in Burnett County, and to act without any further orders. To arrest all deserters and "bushwhackers" and to " kill every —— —— Indian that puts his foot in the County." Here the Captain smiled, and replied: "Well, Colonel, that 'foot' order pleases me, for every light moon in this year of '63 our county has been raided by a band of Indians and one of their number has a remarkably big foot; it is generally believed by all that have seen his tracks that he is a man of powerful physique, and is the chief of his tribe, and I long to measure lances with him to decide our prowess as soldiers of different nationalities."

With a smile of approval and a manly shake of the hand, the Colonel said: "Go, and God be with you and give victory to the right."

The Captain lost no time in going home and organizing the company as he was ordered, and none too soon, for three days after the organization, Big Foot and his band made a raid into Captain Jeff's settlement, and stole most of the best work horses and mules, and Big Foot had the audacity to go into the orchards and gather fruit so that his tracks could be seen by any one as a banter, "catch me if you can." Could his ears have been properly opened, a "still small voice" would have whispered to him "Captain Jeff lives, and he will live until you have to meet him face to face. You may leave misery and desolation in your path, for many moons, or even years, but the fates have decreed that he shall hunt you down at last, and while your spirit is taking its departure from this earth, where you have caused so much suffering and sorrow, he will be riding at the head of his gallant Ranger boys to carry the news that Big Foot's raids are at an end, and that he met the reward that was decreed to him by Fate."

The next morning by early breakfast couriers began to arrive at Captain Jeff's with the exciting news that last night Big Foot had raided the entire neighborhood and stolen several of the neighbors' best horses and mules.

The Captain at once dispatched the couriers in different directions to notify his company to rendezvous at a certain point in which the Indian trails led off and to bring as much bread as they could conveniently carry, and some salt. This was the standing order for rations ever afterwards. So by noon of that day, seventeen men were at the appointed spot, and took the traill and pressed it with all possible speed through the roughs and breaks of the Colorado River and across the San Saba River.

But as Big Foot and band had good fat, corn-fed horses to change upon, they gained rapidly upon their pursurers, and, after four days of hard persuit, the word "halt" was given; the trail was abandoned and Captain Jeff's cherished hope of a deadly encounter with Big Foot was deferred to an indefinite time.

The dazed and worried expressions of the men's faces for six long days as they wended their way back, was distressing indeed, they having accomplished nothing but to find out and fully locate the trail that Big Foot and band had in the last twelve months driven thirteen droves of horses across the same crossing of the San Saba River. After ten days they reached home, horses and men badly jaded, as the men had not eaten anything for the last six days but meat, salt and water.

Before the Captain disbanded his men he told them to get their horses in as good shape as possible, and to have everything in readiness for the next light moon, for said he: "The next time Big Foot raids this county I will beat him to that crossing on the San Saba, and there lie in wait and snuff out his light, or die in the attempt, God helping me."

So with sullen and sad countenances they bid each other adieu for the time being, not knowing that they were destined to realize more such sad experiences before the wily Big Foot, chief of the Kiowa tribe, was outgeneraled by his determined adversary, as the sequel will prove.

When the Captain made the vow to his men that the next time Big Foot made a raid he would beat him to that crossing on the San Saba, or die in the attempt, he did not know how soon he would be called upon to fulfill that vow, nor the trying circumstances under which it was to be performed.

As he had a fine stock of horses and the Indians were getting more or less of them every light moon, he decided to gather them and drive them to Caldwell County below the line of Indian raids. So, the last day he gathered horses was on Sunday. He rode hard all that day and got home just at sundown, unsaddled his horse and staked him out as he had no feed to feed him, and got back to the house and ate his supper after which he and his wife walked out and took chairs on the gallery.

# CHAPTER II.

Indian Depredations Come Thick and Fast and the Big Foot Indian Kiowa Chief, the Most Formidable Enemy of the Frontier, and his Wonderful Seeming Providential Escapes.

The Captain's first lieutenant, John Owens, rode up to the front gate and reported that the Indians had just killed Wafford Johnson and family about one mile south of the Captain's house.

He at once went and brought up his tired horse, threw the saddle on and mounted him, without any protest by his brave and noble wife at being left alone, and as he rode off she said: "Jeff, go and avenge the death of those noble and good people, and may God bless you and bring you safe back to me and the children."

Such was the woman worthy to be the wife of the man who was destined to rid the bleeding frontier of the State of Texas of the two most barbarous and bloody savages that ever depredated upon it, namely: Big Foot, the Kiowa Chief, and Jape, the Comanche, his first lieutenant.

As Captain Jeff and Lieut. Owens rode off from the Captain's house he said: "Now, Lieut. Owens, our physical abilities will be put to the strain, I have ridden forty miles today, we will be compelled to ride as much as forty miles tonight to get our company rendezvoused in marching order at the spot where the Johnson family were killed. It is ninety miles from there to the noted crossing of the San Saba River, and you know at the termination of our last scout I made a vow that I would beat the next Indians that raided us to that crossing, or die, God helping me. Lieut. Owens, I will perform that feat."

The first house they reached was Alex Barton's. He had one good horse at his house, three other good ones in his field.

He quickly saddled his horse to accompany them in calling the company together, remarking as he threw on the saddle: "I will ride Kate to-night, and get one of my horses out of the field in the morning to ride on the scout. Poor fellow, he did not know what the morning held in store for him.

Captain Jeff, Lieut. Owens and Barton rode all night notifying and giving orders for the members of the Company to assemble at the point designated, at as early hour as possible, with arms, bread and salt. At about four o'clock in the morning as these three were returning they had to cross the San Gabriel creek, one bank of which made a part of Barton's field fence.

The crossing on the creek was near the steep bank that made a part of Barton's fence, and it was very bushy, and just as they reached that point the Captain said, "Stop boys, the Indians are right here." They suddenly halted, looked wildly around, and as they did not see nor hear the Indians, they commenced to laugh. The Captain remarked: "You need not laugh, the Indians are right here, or very near here, for I smell them; this is not the first time I have smelt Indians of a night when they could not be seen, and have proved it to the men that were with me at the time." So when daylight dawned and Barton went out into his field to get his fresh horse to ride on the scout, the revelations proved that at the time our party crossed the creek and Captain Jeff said that he smelt them, they (the Indians) had Barton's horses rounded up on the high bank in the field where they caught them. They went around and let down the fence and crossed the creek at the same crossing that our party had just crossed. On examination of the tracks it was plainly evident that Big Foot got Barton's horses. One of Barton's horses was a very fine mare, gentle to handle, but not broke to ride, and just after crossing the creek where the Captain smelt them, one of them tried to ride her and she threw him, evidence of which the marks on the ground disclosed; and they killed her then and there to let the hated pale faces know that if they could not use her no one else should.

Had Big Foot been a few minutes longer in getting to the crossing of the creek he would have met his sworn and determined enemy but it seems that the time was not full ripe for the final contest, so we go forward and chronicle the events just as they transpire. The Captain reached his home that morning just at day light and found his noble wife preparing his breakfast with the full hope that he would be there in due time to take breakfast with her, and rest for only a few minutes. The children had not yet awakened, so he softly went to the bed and kissed their sweet and innocent faces, sat down and partook of a hearty breakfast, put his arms around his wife, kissed her, and gently patting her on the shoulder told her to be of good cheer, that in due time he would return;

that he had full faith and hope that "God would protect the right." So saying he walked out and mounted his tired horse and urged him forward for one more mile to the spot where Wafford Johnson and family fell brutally murdered by Big Foot and his savage band.

In twenty minutes from the time he left home his horse that had carried him seventy or eighty miles in the last twenty-four hours carried him to the tragic spot of the evening before.

When he reached the place but two or three of his men were there in his advance. Dismounting, he walked to a pool of blood where Johnson had lain in the road. There was Big Foot's tracks plainly to be seen where he had bent over Johnson's body to take off his pistol belt and scabbord.

In looking further over the ground, the road ran close by a dense dogwod thicket, in which a noise was heard, and on further examination of the cause of the noise, it was found that Mrs. Johnson as she ran her horse close by the thicket, threw her baby boy of one year old in the thicket, with a mother's never dying love to the last, that he might escape discovery by the Indians, and be found by some friendly hand that would kindly take care of her darling baby boy. The poor little fellow lay where he fell in the thicket all night, a prey to the wild beasts of the jungle, with an arrow through his right arm.

His uncle soon came on the ground, and took the little sufferer to where he could get nourishment and attention. The circumstances of the killing of Johnson are supposed to be these:

A Mr. Whitehead, lived about a mile from Johnson. On Sunday morning Johnson and family, consisting of wife and three children, visited Mr. Whitehead where they remained until late in the day when they started home horseback. Mrs. Johnson rode with her oldest girl beind her and her baby boy in her lap; Johnson rode another horse and carried his second daughter, a beautiful little girl of four summers, in his lap. She was his idolized pet. She and Johnson must have been killed when the attack was first made, for when found he had his left arm around her, his right arm had been used to defend her to the last moment.

The oldest girl who rode behind Mrs. Johnson, jumped off the horse and was not discovered by the Indians, and she ran home, which was only some three hundred yards from where the attack was made. Mrs. Johnson's horse ran some one hundred yards before she fell, her body filled with arrows. Reader, my pen utterly fails to portray to you my fellings while I have to chronicle the short details of this foul murder that was blacker than hell itself.

All that we could say was: "Go on, Big Foot, your day of retribution must, shall and will come."

By the time the sun was one hour high the company, to the number of thirty men, had assembled. The Captain selected fifteen men with the best horses, and put the other fifteen on the trail and told them to follow it for six days, and he offered one hundred dollars reward to the man that killed the Indian that carried Wafford Johnson's pistol.

The Captain's horse was completely exhausted for the time being, but an old man by the name of Baker offered him his horse, which was a good one, which he thankfully accepted. The change of saddles was quickly made, and mounting Mr. Baker's horse, he said to the fifteen men he had selected: "All that think they can ride ninety miles in the next twenty-six or twenty-eight hours, follow me; for, God helping me, I will ride it if I get there alone, and block Big Foot's passage across the San Saba River and kill him if I can, or be killed." He led off and all the fifteen followed him. They rode steadily forward until noon; halted, and let their horses crop a few mouthsful of grass while they ate a hasty lunch. In thirty minutes they were again in their saddles, pressing forward, and continued to do so until after dark when they came to a ranch house where they got a feed of corn for their horses, and while the horses were eating the men also ate their supper. Here the rest was prolonged for an hour, at the expiration of which time they were again in their saddles and pressing forward to the noted Indian crossing on the San Saba River. They rode steadily on until the new day was breaking when the Captain said "halt" as they were in a nice place to take a rest and let their tired horses rest and eat grass for an hour while they ate a lunch themselves.

At sunrise they were again in their saddles pressing forward, and in half an hour they struck the noted Indian trail that led through narrow gaps in the mountains to the crossing of the San Saba River. The Captain was in the lead when they struck the trail. He raised his hat and smilingly said: "Come on, boys!" and rode straight forward across the trail, which the men thought was a strange procceding, for they thought he would follow the trail.

He rode steadily forward for one mile, when he halted, and when the men all came up he explained to them what they thought was strange in him in riding straight across the trail.

He said: "Boys, when we struck the trail I could hardly keep from hollowing, for I saw if Big Foot is aiming to cross the San Saba at his regular crossing that we are ahead of him and time to spare; and if he is coming on the trail behind us, had we taken the trail when he struck our fresh horse tracks ahead of him he would have turned his course and crossed somewhere else.

So it is good luck for us, but puts us under the painful necessity of riding several miles further in making a circle several miles further around to the crossing." They all agreed that he had taken the proper course.

They rode steadily forward making a circle of the crossing and reached it in twenty-eight hours from the time of starting, making ninety-five miles in twenty eight hours without change of horses or a wink of sleep. And now with dispatch every thing was put in proper shape to accomplish what they had ridden so hard for, should the opportunity present itself in the coming of Big Foot and his band. Two men were sent back to an elevated spot that commanded the trail for some distance, and Captain Jeff felt sanguine that he, after another hard effort, had set the trap that Big Foot would walk into.

As nothing further could be arranged or perfected, Liuet. Owens insisted that Captain Jeff lie down and take a short sleep, for said he: "No man living can stand up longer than you have; you have ridden one hundred and sixty-five miles without one wink of sleep. An iron will and a nerve of steel can not stand any more, and when the critical moment does come, we want you at your best; so lay down and sleep just two hours, and I will wake you up, and then I will lie down and sleep till you wake me up." Feeling sure that everything was so arranged that should the Indians come while he was asleep that they could not escape, he lay down and in two minutes he was sound asleep, for the utmost of man's endurance had been reached.

As all the men had been instructed to sleep two hours alternately, Lieut. Owens let the Captain sleep three hours, when he woke him. And when the Captain had bathed his face with a canteen of pure spring water that had just been brought from a cold spring that gushed out of the bluff on the river, he said: "Lieut., I feel very much refreshed, and am in much better shape to tackle that Big Foot Indian than when I got here. At all events, I wish he would put in his appearance and let us decide the contest that must be decided sooner or later, and he is not in sight yet. I want you to lie down and sleep until I wake you, for I want you to stand guard with me tonight a quarter of a mile from camp on the trail."

At six o'clock there was no sign of the Indians, and Captain Jeff roused up all the men and told them to prepare supper, so they could eat and put out all the fire before dark, which was done. And no Indians yet! Everything was properly arranged at the crossing and the Captain took Lieut. Owens and went back on the trail to a big liveoak tree that stood some three or four feet from the trail. They sat down with their backs to the tree where they had full view of the trail for some distance.

About twelve o'clock they saw something coming down the trail, and as it came nearer, they saw that it was an old buck (deer). Captain Jeff put his hand to his side and slowly drew his big Bowie knife and slipped his arm slowly up the tree, and when the big buck got just opposite to where he sat, he threw the knife with lightning speed and its point went straight to the mark. The buck bounded high in the air, and fell on his back dead, with the knife driven to the handle square through his heart.

Lieut. Owens remarked: "Captain, that was well done. I think Providence sent us that buck, for we are almost famished for meat, and we are not allowed to shoot any for fear of driving off the game of which we are in pursuit." They lifted the buck off of the trail, extracted the knife from the heart, opened him with it and took out his intestines and turned him over so that all the blood would drain out. They had brought two canteens of water with them to use through the night. Captain Jeff said: "Lieut., we will use one of these to wash our hands for we can afford to be short on water, to be long on such meat as this, for we are almost famished for one square meal, and tomorrow we will have it, Big Foot or no Big Foot," after which conversation they took their respective stations at the big tree and sat out their lonely and silent vigil through the remainder of the night, and no Indians yet.

When daylight was fully come they fastened their buck's legs together, hunted up a suitable pole which they slipped through them and each one took an end of the pole and they bore him into camp in the same manner that Moses' spies brought grapes from the Promised Land. When they reached camp there was much wonder and surprise among the boys as to how such a fine deer could be captured without the use of fire arms. Lieut. Owens replied: "We got him as Abraham got the ram for his sacrifice, or in equally as miraculous a manner. It was sent to us as an offering for breakfast, and if you all feel like I do, the offering is truly and thankfully received."

As the camp was in good shape, the men rested. The only thing necessary to make each of them half horse and half aligator was just one more square meal, and that was plainly in sight.

As Captain Jeff had only slept three hours in the last three days and nights, sleep was absolutely necessary before food. He therefore turned the command of the company over to Lieut. Owens for the next six hours. He placed a rock against a tree for a pillow, spread down his saddle blanket for a bed, told the boys that he was going to sleep for six hours, and he hoped they would leave enough of the buck for him a square meal when he was waked at twelve o'clock, whereupon he stretched himself on his downy couch, and was in the land of forgetfulness in two minutes.

Ah, Sleep! Sleep, sweet sleep! What a boon to us mortals! The iron will, the nerve of steel must succumb in the absence of its life and health-giving influence!

While Captain Jeff sleeps to gain strength for any emergency that might arise, and all the rest are put on guard or picket duty except two, who are detailed to cook, let us take a peep into how Texas Rangers can cook good bread and get up a good meal without any semblance of a cooking vessel.

The first our cooks do is to make a good fire out of dry wood, and while it is burning down into good coals, they proceeded to strip the hide off the buck; they then wash all the blood off the hide and hang it up for a few minutes to drip. They then spread it down and put the flour, salt and soda in sufficient quantities to make it light and pliable, they then cut up fine a quantity of the inside fat and put in sufficient water and knead it well, using the hide as a bread pan. They then get some nice straight sticks three or four feet long, the size of a man's thumb, peel off the bark, sharpen one end. They then take some of the dough and wrap it around the blunt end of the stick for one foot in length or more, and stick the sharp end in the ground leaning it the proper angle over the fire, so it will cook to a finish, the inside fat that was cut up in the flour equally distributed the grease all through the bread, and better bread could not be cooked anywhere or in anyway. They cook the meat with the same stick process, only both ends of the stick are sharpened and the stick is forced half way through the piece of meat and the sharp ends of the stick alternately turned and stuck in the ground, as the case may require. In this manner a savory meal was gotten up, and all the men in turn got a meal never to be forgotten.

They ate and thanked kind Providence that sent them the fine buck, went and relieved those who stood on guard, and' they came and did likewise.

By the time all had been boutifully fed, Captain Jeff had slept his six hours, and Lieut. Owens awoke him and poured water out of a canteen while he washed and bathed his face and head, after which he said: "I am as hungry as a bear," and casting his eyes towards the fire he said that his boys in their feast had not forgotten him, for there on a stick was one full side of ribs of the big buck, cooked to a turn and two stickes of as good bread as was ever eaten; and one of the cooks coming up with a canteen of pure, cold spring water. The Captain sat down and did not rise until the last rib was picked and the last mouthful of bread was eaten. He rose, picked up the canteen and washed it all down with a quart of the cold spring water; he then began humming:

"The Big Foot Indian, with his pretty little squaw,
He can't feel better than I do now;"

after which he filled his big pipe, lit it, sat down, leaned back against a tree a perfect picture of physical manhood and contentment. After he had finished his pipe, he got up and began to walk the camp. Stopping suddenly where some of the men were lounging on the grass, he said: "Boys, these things are getting very monotonous to me, and I reasonably suppose it is to you, but let us bear it with all the patience we can for twenty-four hours more; we may yet be rewarded for our perseverance, vigilance and patience.'"

The same routine of duties were kept up until nine o'clock the next day, and no Indians yet, at which time a man strode into camp heavily armed with two army six-shooters and a government musket. His appearance caused every man to rise to his feet. His general appearance fully denoted that he was a son of "old Erin's green Isle." ' He saluted the party with "Gude morning, gintlemen, and is this Captain Giff's camp?" (to which he was answered in the affirmative), "and, thin, is the gintleman prisent?" The Captain stepped forward and said, "I am the man." "Will, thin, yer honor, I have bin sint here to inform ye that the Ingins crost the river six miles beyant here two days ago." "Pat are you sure the Indians crossed the river six miles above here two days ago?" "I am, sor, for don't ye think the domn bludy bugar of a Big Fute chafe was musket," at which the boys set up a laugh that reverberated after following me about four miles up the river, and he fired a ball at me, and it struck jist firninst me hale; and I didn't have a domn thing to defind meself wid but these two large six-shooters and the for miles up and down the San Saba river. The Captain joined in the laugh with the boys and made a full hand. After the merriment had somewhat subsided, the Captain said: "Pat, had you been armed, you would have 'mixed' it with the chief, wouldn't you?" to which Pat replied, "And sure I would, sor." "And what sort of arms did you want, Pat?" "I think, sor, the way that big chafe looked while he was chasing me up the river, that I wanted about three Gatlin guns that could shoot 990 times in a minute, sor; why, sor, he is the biggest mon ye ever saw, and his fute is two fate long." Just at this juncture a bunch of cattle came down the trail. The Captain drew his big six-shooter and shot down a fat yearling, and said: "Boys, dress that fellow and barbecue him as soon as you can, and we will leave this camp of disappointment just as soon as that is done." Pat picked up his gun that had been standing by a tree, threw it on his shoulder, and said: "Well, gintlemen, I'll be after bidding yous the time of day, and gude luck to yous all." The Captain said: "Why, Pat, you ain't a-going to leave before dinner? We are going to have a fine barbecued beef for dinner." He replied: "Thank ye, sor; I have a lunch wid me, and I'd rather make my journey while yous are here than to make it when yous are gone," and he walked off. When he reached the river bank the Captain called after him: "I say, Pat, you'd better get you one of them Gatlin guns, for you don't know when you may meet that Big Foot fellow." Pat stopped, faced around, and replied: "And sure you are right, yer honor, and I'll be after gettin' me one at me first convenience." He turned and stepped down the bank, and was never seen any more, but he had the sympathies of all that knew him in his supposed tragic death.

By two o'clock the meat was well barbecued, and the orders were given to pack up, and the homeward march was begun. They rode silently and sullenly, with a dazed expression of countenance, for they fully realized that the opportunity to meet the big chief in deadly conflict was to be deferred to some indefinite time, for by this time he and his band were safely housed in his mountain fastness, surrounded by his many braves, his many wives and numerous papooses.

# CHAPTER III.

**The Disobedience of Orders and the Timidity of the Women, Doubtless Prolonged the Wily Chief's Existance.**

They reached home the third day after they broke camp, and nothing worthy of note had transpired during their absence. They found their families all well, and no report of Indians. The next morning Captain Jeff mounted his horse and rode around to inquire why his orders had been disobeyed, and why the fifteen men that he had put on the trail with orders to folow it six days, failed to do so. Their only excuse was, they had no one to leave with their wives, who refused to be left alone. Mark the contrast between those women and the wife of our hero on the same occasion, when she kissed him good-bye, and said: "Jeff, go and avenge the death of those good and noble people." Had other wives been possessed of the same spirit, the opportunity was then offered to overtake Big Foot and mete out to him the punishment he so justly deserved for the base murder of so many defenseless women and children. In this instance, in place of Big Foot going out of the neighborhood the same direction he went many times before, that went to the crossing on the San Saba river, after some ten miles he tacked back due south through the cedar brakes of Burnet County, went north through Llano County and killed two men that were ploughing, and leisurely went on and crossed the San Saba river six miles above where Captain Jeff had been lying in wait for him twenty-four hours in his advance.

The disobedience of orders in all probability prolonged the wily chief's existence to an indefinite time to commit many more horrible crimes on defenseless women and children.

After this raid Burnet County had immunity from the visits of Indians for three light moons, and the constant and daily fear began to somewhat subside. At the expiration of this time Captain Jeff had retired for the night, when a "Hello!" was heard at his front gate. He sprang out of bed, opened the door and inquired, "What is wanting?" His caller informed him that the Indians were in, and that the settlement would be raided that night. He quickly donned his clothes, kissed his wife an affectionate "bye-bye," as if he were going to a picnic, went and saddled his horse, and as he rode by the gate, she hollered after him: "Jeff, I hope you will catch that big rascal this time." This was the kind of metal that rescued the bleeding frontier from the merciless savages and made it a fit abode for those that came after them, and they were never honored for their hardships, dangers and privations incident thereto.

We return to follow Captain Jeff after he left his home on this occasion. His experience had taught him that it was almost impossible to trail the Indians and overtake them, therefore it was necessary to get ahead of them and lie in wait at some noted pass that was known to be their passway; so thinking the matter over as he rode, he found that nine of his men lived in the direction or partial direction of one of the Indians' noted pass-ways. He therefore pressed forward to the first and roused him up, and he saddled his horse, got his arms and started with him, and they two rode to the next house, where the same program was carried out, and so on until the nine men were in their saddles and pressing forward to the noted Spy Mountain pass, thirty miles from the Captain's home, which they reached by hard riding at six o'clock in the morning.

They had no provisions with them, only what little cold bread that was left at their different homes the evening before and a little sack of salt that Captain Jeff always carried in his saddle pocket so as to have salt in an emergency, for good beef could be obtained at any time or place, with nothing but the trouble to pick out the size wanted and kill it, for the Captain's Company held a carte-blanche to use beef out of any mark or brand when in pursuit of Indians. So, when reaching Spy Mountain, they found that they were ahead of the Indians.

A buch of cattle was grazing near by. The Captain ordered Bill Donivan, who was an expert roper, to rope a fat calf for breakfast, for their appetites were whetted to a razor edge, after their hard ride through the night. Captain Jeff had ridden fifty or sixty miles from ten o'clock at night to six o'clock that morning, the zig-zag course taken to collect his men. The calf was soon roped, killed and dressed.

Two men were put on Spy Mountain to watch for the approach of the Indians. The horses were tied behind a thicket that hid them from view, with their saddles and bridles on, so that they could be mounted at a moment's warning. Everything was put in perfect readiness to welcome the Indians with hospitable hands to bloody graves should they come.

As yet no indications from the spies. The Captain told his men to cut and broil beef to suit themselves; he chose for his part a half side of ribs. So in less time than it takes to write it, sticks were cut and run through pieces of meat, Ranger style, and stuck up around the fire that had been built at the start so as to have the coals in readiness. The men were not forgotten that were on guard, and two big, fine hunks were put up to roast for them. The meat was soon cooked to a rare state just to suit the taste of a Texas Ranger. All the cold bread was brought forward, which was ample for one meal, and this meal of cold bread and broiled beef was enjoyed as much as any meal that was ever eaten at the famous Delmonico restaurant in the city of New York. After they had finished their meal the spies were kept up alternately every two hours through the entire day until near sundown, the horses standing just as they were placed, without feed or drink the entire day, which was really hard on the poor, faithful creatures, but the necessity required it, and it had to be done.

Just as the sun was setting the spies discovered a lone horseman coming through the gap in the mountain the Indians were expected to come through, which was quickly reported, and every man mounted his horse and stood ready to receive the report of the lone horseman, who soon came up with the speed of a frightened deer. It proved to be Rheuben Senterfit, well-known to all our party as a fearless rider, and he was mounted on a superb West Texas horse that had the wind and sure foot equal to any horse in the world. He reined up his horse and said: "Boys, I knew you were here, and I have ridden for life to be in at the killing. The Indians left the trail south of the gap and have gone south of you." At that moment he looked in a southwesterly direction, and said: "There go the damn rascals now! Boys, look on the top of that bald hill," which was a mile or more distant from where they stood. He led, with all the others close at his horse's heels, in this race, the most headlong and furious riding that the writer has ever witnessed.

Their speed soon brought them to the top of the hill that they saw the Indians go over. Here they halted, and Senterfit's dog struck the trail and gave them the direction they had gone. They looked and discovered them below the base of the mountain, some half a mile distant, or more. They were riding like dare-devils, driving a bunch of about forty horses, over ground that didn't look safe to ride over in a wallk.

The plunge down that mountain in pursuit was fearful indeed. They reached its base in safety, and on and on, with the same headlong speed, over honey-comb rock that did not seem possible for horses to be driven over faster than a walk. The Indians saw that they were hotly and closely pursued, when one of them cried out, "Jeffa! Jeffa! Jeffa!" at which time they abandoned the horses they were driving and rode for life. That "Jeffa"—"Jefa," "Jefa," as they pronounced it—struck double terror to their hearts and, if possible, lent power to their exertions for safety.

But our pursuers of nine men gained steadily upon the nine savages, and when there was only a space of forty yards between the pursuers and the pursued two shots rang out, and at that instant the savages disappeared as if the earth had opened and swallowed them, all but two horses that were standing stock still on the spot where the pursued had disapepared.

The writer here wishes to explain the wherefore of this strange occurrence. Just as the two shots range out from Captain Jeff's party the Indians' horses had reached the very brink of a perpendicular bank of a deep ravine, whose banks were all of ten feet high or deep; its bottom was covered with a dense growth of small native timber, and its real presence would not be discovered until you were on its very brink, particularly if you were riding fast and going directly to it.

The two shots fired as mentioned may have lent an additional impetus to both the Indians and their horses in making such a headlong leap; be that as it may, the leap was successfully made, and just at that propitious moment for the Indians, the darkness of night spread her black mantle over the scene and heavy rain commenced pouring down.

The writer here wishes to ask, "Was this occurrence, and many more similar to it, yet to be recorded in this little narrative of facts, (yes, positive facts, that are recorded just as they occurred) providential?" Truly, I ask, "Were the Indians on this occasion protected by a special Providence, and many similar occasions, as the further perusal of this narrative will show?"

When the pursuers reached the bank of the canyon where the two horses stood, they could plainly hear Big Foot giving orders to his men in a loud, clear, Indian voice. It would have been poor generalship under the adverse circumstances to have climbed down that bluff, where all would have been killed without ever having seen an Indian. They would have picked off each man as he climbed down a tree, as there was no other way of descent except to jump down, which last method might have caused some broken or badly strained legs; there was nothing else to do but make virtue out of pressing necessity to provide for the famished and jaded horses, only to draw off to a safe distance from the Indians' arms and to camp for the night.

A beautiful little rivulet wound its way into the main canyon, up which he went some fourth of a mile, where he found good grass and water for his famished horses. Here they were unsaddled and picketed out, and five men, the Captain as one, formed a circle or cordon around the horses, and the other four men spread down their saddle blankets on the wet ground with their saddles for a pillow. They were so fatigued that they were soon asleep and dreaming pleasant dreams in place of the exciting scenes that had just been passed through.

At one o'clock the sleepers were roused up, and took the places of the Captain and his guard, who in turn took their places on the pallets and were fast asleep in two minutes, which sleep was absolutely necessary for the trials that lay before them for the morrow. At daylight all were up, saddled their horses and rode to where the Indians made the leap, and the two poor horses that they could not force over the bluff had not moved off more than fifty yards. They were literally whipped (some parts of them) almost to a jelly. Here the Captain led his men down the canyon some hundred yards to where the bluff terminated and where there was a crossing, and here they struck the Indians' trail. After following it some three hundred yards, it passed a man's house by the name of Allen, who was coming towards them. When he got close enough to speak, he said, "Boys, what's up?" The reply was: "We are after Indians. We ran them into that deep canyon last night; didn't you hear two shots just as it commenced to rain?" He replied: "Yes, I was right here, and hobbled out two good horses just as the shots were fired." In looking around a little, they picked up a nice rawhide larjat, and there, plain to be seen, was Big Foot's track in the sand, where he had roped Allen's horses. Here let us recount the luck, the Providence, or the what not, that befell these Indians in the last twelve hours. First, they went around the pass that they had always gone through, where Captain Jeff had them surely bagged if they had gone through. Second, when they were run down and overtaken, we may say that the earth opened to protect them and the horses, all but the two that they could not force into the chasm, and they were worthless to them, as they were completely run down. Third, that in going six hundred yards from where two of them had to turn a somersault over their horses' heads down into the deep canyon, two good horses were hobbled out and in waiting for them. There was no management or generalship in these transactions. Reader, you are at liberty to call it what you please.

"The prospects to overtake these Indians, when freshly mounted, is slim," Captain Jeff remarked, as he was hesitating what to do. The Captain's horses were badly jaded after the hard run putting the Indians into the deep canyon, and had thrown every shoe in the six-mile run over the honey-comb rocks.

After a moment's hesitation, the Captain said: "Boys, the prospect to overtake Big Foot on these horses is gloomy indeed. We have no show whatever to get fresh ones, but I am loth to abandon his trail without one more desperate and determined effort to bring him to bay where he must fight for his liberty instead of running for it. Some small voice seems to speak to me every time that I have run him, that his good luck will forsake him and fall on me, and that I will be the victor, and this may be the day. If you will follow me, we will urge our horses to their utmost in trying to overtake him." The unanimous reply from the eight men was: "Captain Jeff, we will follow you to the end of the world to kill that big brute," to which the Captain said: "He has eight men, and he makes nine; you are eight, and I make nine; so our numbers are equal, and should we overtake them, each one of you single out your man. Remember, this time for all, that I claim the honor to be his special antagonist until one of us fall."

The Captain turned his horse to the trail, and the rest followed, and the race for the day began. They had followed the trail about four miles, when they came to a fine horse belonging to an old man by the name of Wolf, one of the Captain's remote neighbors, but near neighbor to some of his men. Here they found Big Foot's tracks again where he had lassoed another fine horse that seemed to have been placed directly on the route, and just at the spot that old man Wolf's horse gave out. Our wily chief had made four lucky hits in the last few hours, which, no doubt, inspired a greater confidence in his braves and led them to believe that he was a particular favorite of the Great Spirit, and that he could lead or bring them out of all difficulties that they might encounter while making war on the palefaces. This last piece of good luck for the Indians added an additional gloom to the already gloomy prospects of overtaking them that day, but they were determined to follow until their horses gave out. The trail was fresh until about noon, when they came to where the Indians had killed a big mooly cow and had taken most of her meat, and her paunch to carry water in. Here was a thick grove of trees, a nice place to secrete themselves. They tied their horses to the trees, so that they could be mounted at a moment's warning, and lay down in the grass and slept; their beds were all plainly to be seen very near their horses.

The calf of the cow which the Indians had killed was standing near by; it was fine and fat, and as the Captain's party had not tasted food since the day before, the cravings of hunger demanded that they should stop, kill that calf and eat it, while their horses rested and grazed for a short time, if the trail was to be pursued any further. They at once lassoed the calf and carried out the program of resting and eating, which was fully carried out for two hours from the time they stopped, which was all the time they could take from the trail if it was to be pursued any further.

After this the horses were saddled and the unanimous voice was to follow, as there was one chance in a thousand that the Indians had taken so much meat that should a favorable spot present itself they would stop and barbecue the beef.

They pressed forward all the evening through breaks, canyons and bluffs of the Colorado river with the hope of soon coming in sight of the smoke of the Indians' fire. At sundown they found that they were compelled to camp for the night, as their horses could go no further, and on making a very careful examination of the locality it was found to be a spot that looked like it was formed by nature for a camping place for this very occasion. It looked as much like a providential arrangement around us as one of Big Foot's escapades, and as he had not taken the advantage of camping in this strategic spot all hope of overtaking him with these completely broken-down horses fled. Here was plenty of grass and water, and the place so walled in by natural fortifications that two men could hold it indefinitely against fifty Indians.

The horses were all turned foot-loose, two men on guard, one at the inlet and one at the outlet; all the rest lay down at once to sleep. They had eaten but one meal in twenty-four hours, but they were more sleepy than hungry. The two men on guard changed guards alternately every two hours; and all therefore got a good night's sleep and rest.

At daylight all were up and ready for any emergency that might arise. At this time the most pressing emergency that forcibly presented itself was to appease the cravings of hunger that were loudly knocking and craving to be gratified.

There was but one door open for such gratification, which was the usual one—to kill a beef and make a meal of beef, salt and water, which was partaken of without a murmur for something better. After the meal was concluded preparations were made to take the back track, but on examination it was found that the horses were so footsore they could not travel. The Captain ordered the men to cut up the beef hide and make a kind of a rawhide moccasin and tie the same around the fetlock so as to come under the bottoms of their feet, which was done, and they rested all that day at Camp Providence, or Camp Good Luck.

Nothing worthy of note transpired that day or night. The following morning they got up their horses and saddled them and started for home. It was then found that most of the horses' feet were so sore that the men had to walk and drive them to get them home, which journey was accomplished in five days without any incident worthy of record, only the worry and fatigue of walking and driving the worn-out horses that distance.

At home they found all well, and no report of Indians during their absence. They went to work with a will as best they could to be in readiness for the next raid, which was as sure as fate to come, since it was only a matter of time.

For many moons the Indians gave Burnet County a wide berth, for they had found that Burnet County was too hot for them; that they would surely have to "run the gauntlet" if they made tracks in that county. Big Foot changed his location to depredate upon.

The next raid he made was on the west line of Burnet County and east line of Llano County. He killed Mrs. Blalock and four of her children, which report Captain Jeff did not get for several days, when it was too late to follow. On this raid Big Foot, in addition to killing the Blalock family, stole and got away with forty or fifty good horses.

The next raid was still further west, through Mason County, where they killed Tom Miligan, a worthy citizen, and father of a large family. They shot him full of arrows within fifty yards of his own house. They then went on and captured Miss Todd, who was going to one of the neighbor's on horseback. They got away with twenty-five or thirty good horses and carried Miss Todd into a captivity a thousand times worse than honorable death.

At the time the Indians made this raid Captain Jeff had been ordered by Colonel Ford to meet him with his company on the Colorado river fifty miles above Austin city for the breaking up of some bands of bushwhackers and deserters. The country here along this river is very rough and abounds in many caves that were found to be full of the above class of men, and as some of them fought to desperation they necessarily had to be killed (mention of which will be made before this recital is closed).

Many prisoners were taken, whom Colonel Ford took to the city of Austin and placed in confinement, and then he ordered Captain Jeff and company back home.

# CHAPTER IV.

**The Civil War has Ended. Gen. Lee has Surrendered and Our Captain Jeff is Hounded as a Wolf by Federal Soldiers, in which the Heroism of a True Woman and Noble Wife Is Illustrated.**

Shortly after this the Civil War ended, and Captain Jeff and company were disbanded, as all other men that had been in any way connected with the Civil War. The State of Texas was then put under military rule, and E. J. Davis was appointed Military Governor, who proved to be a perfect tyrant, and the citizens were subjected to many insults and hardships under his tyrannical rule. Federal soldiers were sent into Burnet County to arrest Professor Holland, Captain Jeff and fifty-eight others who had been conspicuous in hunting down the Indians, bushwhackers and deserters, and Captain Jeff came in for a full share of the persecution that was meted out to the good citizens of Burnet County. Here the Federal soldiers hunted Captain Jeff like a wolf, and he was compelled to take to the brush and make that his home for months. Here the devotion and bravery of his noble wife shone forth with the brilliancy of the morning star.

During this distressing time she had all the burdens to carry that were necessary to keep up their home—wood to get, cows to milk, stock to atend to, and, the hardest burden of all, every other day she had to leave her two little children alone, mount her faithful pony, take some circuitous route to some big thicket with something for her Jeff to eat. Oh, this was the most trying time to those good people that they had to encounter during the almost five years since the commencement of the Civil War. One day she took her two children and went to her brother-in-law's, as was agreed upon by her and Jeff, where he was to be in some big thickets that were near Allen's house, and here he says he was the worst scared that he ever was in his life. He was sitting in a thicket; his horse was near him saddled and bridled for use at any moment. He looked towards Allen's house and saw fifteen Indians riding directly towards the same. He said: "Oh, my God! What shall I do? Oh, my noble wife and children!" But his mind was made up in a moment. He sprang on his horse, drew his six-shooter, and said, "Go, Mansfield! (his horse's name) Go, and I will die with them!" He dashed madly forward, and just before they reached the gate they looked back and saw him coming like a hurricane, pistol held high in the air. They shouted at the tops of their voices, "Toncawa! Toncawa!"

A mountain of intense anxiety was lifted off his breast; the Toncawas had come into the neighborhood the day before, but Captain Jeff had not heard it, and when he saw the Indians, he readily thought that they were Big Foot and his band going to Allen's house to murder its inmates.

Reader, I feel that you will join me in thanks to God that this cloud had its silver lining. The Toncawas had a white man to go around as guide to beg watermelons; Mrs. Allen gave them permission to go into the watermelon patch and they ate every one, ripe or green, that was as big as a man's fist. When it was all cleaned up, they mounted their horses and rode off to hunt another patch. Captain Jeff remained at or near Allen's house all that day and night. When his wife was fixing to start home next morning, he said: "Mollie," (that was his wife's name) "I am going home with you." She tried to dissuade him, but he said: "I can't miss this pleasure to ride home with you and the children; the Yankee soldiers don't have horses that can catch Mansfield" (patting his noble horse on the neck). They rode home together, and the scene that met their eyes when they reached home almost beggars description. The doors were all broken open; the beds turned over, trunks broken open and their contents turned out on the floor. The house had been literally ransacked from cellar to garret. His Sharp's rifle, his double barrel shot-gun, a fine pistol, his wife's fine silver-mounted bridle that cost $22.00, and other things too numerous to mention, were all gone.

Front gate was open, all the milk vessels left sitting outside where they drank the milk, smokehouse door open and a big steer inside of it, and this long after General Lee's surrender.

Reader, how do you think you would have felt if you had been in Captain Jeff's shoes, with his pent-up feelings of disgust for a government that allowed its soldiers to commit such low down petty larceny? Captain said: "Mollie, I feel that Providence has been with us this time." She replied: "Well, this don't look like it, does it?" "To the casual eye it does not, but to the spiritual eye it does," said he. She said a little sarcastically, "Oh, Jeff, what do you mean, what are you talking about?" "Let me explain," said he, "how I see it with the spiritual eye, as some may term it; you see that day before yesterday when I came home for a few moments and asked you to get your pony, take the children and go over to Mat Allen's and stay until this morning, so I could be near you, and we could have the pleasure of each other's company, it relieved you for that time of the worry and fear you have had for months.."

1st. Looking back with the spiritual eye, I see or hear some small voice say: "Jeff, go tell your wife to take the children and go over to Mat Allen's."

2nd. I see that had I not done so, you would have been here and subject to all the insults of a degraded company of Yankee soldiers.

3rd. I see that in all probability that you would have killed some of them, and if so they would have you a prisoner under guard at the city of Austin, where, with all your fortitude and courage, you would have pined away and died with anxiety for me and the children.

4th. I see that we are both here with the children; all well, that our roof is over our heads, and that we can get along very well even with our losses, and I accept our absence from home at this time as a providential thing in our behalf." After he closed this speech, she raised her eyes to his and said: "Jeff, I didn't know that you was such an exhorter only in love affairs. I suggest that when you get out of all these troubles and run down Big Foot that you turn preacher; all the women will join your church."

After this little seemingly bit of sarcasm she said: "There are two sides to every question, and since you have argued your side I am more willing to be convinced; therefore I humbly bow my head to the Giver of all good, that I was not here when they were, and when I wanted to say something ugly about them your little lecture on the spiritual eye has driven all the hard words from my tongue, and each moment I am more and more thankful that I was not at home. You gave me a nice double barrel shot-gun when we were first married, and you learned me to shoot with it, and in your absence I leaned on it for a protector. I have always kept it well loaded with buck shot for big game like man, and I fully believe had I been at the house and ordered those Yankee soldiers not to come into it, and they had attempted to do so, that I should have shot and killed some of them, and you correctly drew the picture, that I now would be a prisoner under guard and guarded by those same despoilers of our home, and oh, God! the agonizing thought of being torn from our children, and placed under guard and subject to the daily insults of, I must say brutes in men's clothing! Oh, horrible! horrible! With bowed head and humbleness of spirit I join you in returning thanks to God for overshadowing us by His providence and shielding us from bodily harm through all the trying scenes of the last five years.

When the soldiers broke open Captain Jeff's house they had four of the best men of Burnet County as prisoners. They had them chained and locked to their horses' necks. They were over military age, but were particular friends and associates of Captain Jeff, and they wanted to fix him the same way, for he was reported to them as being the ring leader, and was reported to General Oaks by some of his neighbors that claimed to be Union men, as a murderer and robber, consequently every effort was made to capture him, but kind fate kept him out of their clutches until such time as his protecting voice told him to go and surrender. As the Yankee soldiers had gone on to Austin, Captain Jeff decided that he would stay around home until he heard that the soldiers had come back to Burnet County. His house was a double house, gallery in front, ten foot hall between, two shed rooms back. He fixed one of the shed rooms for his horse and kept him in it all the time with the saddle on, and the bridle hanging on the horn of the saddle so that he could mount him and be gone in a few moments.

So the days came and went for some ten or twelve. When he had eaten his supper and had slept out in the hall one of his neighbor's boys ran by his gate on his horse, and as he passed the gate he said: " Captain Jeff, the Yankee soldiers are coming after you; they are right up there by your field." The bridle was slipped on and the Captain was in his saddle just as quickly as such a performance could be done. As he rode off he said: "Mollie, don't be scared; I will go and meet them, and get them after me and will then lead them off and prevent them from coming to the house to worry you." He dashed out through the field in the direction they were coming, and when he got opposite them, he hollowed and said: "Here I am; come and get me, you —— —— —— ——."

Two of them dismounted, threw down the fence and they all dashed over after him, which was the very thing he wanted, as he had every confidence in the fleetness of his sure-footed horse Mansfield. He led them to the opposite side of the field, and Mansfield leaped the fence without halt or bobble and was gone from his pursuers. After leaping the fence he turned to one side, halted and remained still until they passed him; he then fell in behind them and dodged them until they struck the main road leading to Burnet and they took the road, which satisfied him that they were going on to Burnet that night.

He turned his horse and rode back home. After feeding his

horse and resting a while he said: "Mollie, I have stood this persecution as long as I can; I am going to Austin and give myself up to General Oaks, and ask him to give me justice." She replied: "It is so hard, so hard for me to see you go, but it is no worse than for you to stay here; they will hunt you like a wolf till they do get you, and then chain you on a horse and take you to Austin and throw you into a dungeon as they did Dr. Moore, John Moore, Sam Tate and Captain Dorbant. Taking it all in all, it will be better for you to go and give yourself up than to be arrested by these low down thieves that have just been liberated out of the penitentiaries." He said: "Then I will start at once, ride all night, get into Austin early in the morning, and go at once to General Oaks and surrender myself to him. Be of good cheer, for I feel that I will be safe back home in a few days, in better shape to stay at home than I have been in several months."

He at once mounted his horse, and turned his head towards Austin. Six miles from his home on the road to Austin was the little burg Liberty Hill. The postmaster, Wilson Bratton by name, was a Northern man, and a man of influence, and was a particular friend of Captain Jeff. He hollowed up Bratton as he was passing and told him where he was going. He said: "Captain, go back and give yourself up to the officer at Burnet, and if he puts you under guard, I solemnly pledge you my word of honor that I will never eat, drink or sleep until I release you." "Then I will turn back; it is only twenty miles from here to Burnet; it is now twelve o'clock; I will take through the woods and by six o'clock in the morning I will ride into the soldier camp and give myself up to the officer in command." The Captain then said: "Bratton, 'a friend in need is a friend indeed,' and I here pledge to you my true friendship until death." He heartily shook his hand, and turned his horse through the woods for the soldiers' camp.

# CHAPTER V.

**Captain Jeff Surrenders to the Federal Authorities, in Which the Old Adage Proves True that a "Friend in Need is a Friend Indeed."**

Wilson Bratton was a perfect gentleman, a friend of true men and a merciless foe of frauds; a man whose nobility of soul and mind deserves a monument, but whose name and good deeds have been forgotten, except by those who knew him and benefited by his generosity.

At six o'clock he rode in and recognizing the officer by his uniform, he rode directly up to him and introduced himself to him and said: "I expect you have heard a great many bad things about me." The officer replied: "Yes, I have." The Captain then said: "I can't truthfully be charged with but one thing, and that is being a Rebel, and I have been that to the backbone and I have come into your camp to surrender to you, and all I ask is to get justice." The officer raised his eyes to the Captain's and in a manly voice replied: "You shall have it." Then Captain Jeff said: "I will get down off my horse and consider myself your prisoner." After dismounting he said: "Do you want me to go under guard?" He said: "No, the limits of the camp are yours, but do not attempt to leave it." "I certainly will not without your permission." He then said: "Then I am your friend." After breakfast he issued an order ordering every man in Burnet County to come in and report to him, after which he called his jury of twelve men, all neighbors of Captain Jeff, and during the war they spoke the praises of Captain Jeff on all public occasions and applauded him for the valuable services that he rendered to the frontier after the war was over, and General Oaks was established Military Dictator with headquarters at Austin. See the wolves that had been wearing sheep's clothing, carrying reports to General Oaks that was blacker and more damnable than hell itself, if possible.

These were the men that were selected to sit as jurymen during the examination and cross examination.

**Right here the passage of Scripture was proven that sayeth a man will stick closer to a friend than he will to a brother, in the devotion of Dr. W. E. Jennings to Captain Jeff, and fully illustrated the love of Jonathan for David as recorded in 1st Samuel, 19th and 20th chapters.**

The camp was at a country school house; a sentinel was placed before the door; the jury was called in and the rigid examination and cross-examination of Captain Jeff begun.

The officer had been selected by General Oaks for his fitness as a lawyer and rapid penman, to go to Burnet and get the truth, the whole truth, and nothing but the truth in regard to the many horrible murders that had been committed in Burnet County during the war and had been reported at headquarters by good loyal Union men. The examination lasted three days; the questions all written down and their answers. At the end of the third day the officer had exhausted all his abilities and had not got one solitary criminating fact. He closed his examination and said to his jurymen: "Gentlemen, I am done; I am satisfied; any or all of you are at liberty to ask Captain Jeff any questions you may wish."

Each one got up and said: "I have none," and stepped out with his tail down like a sheep-killing dog, and all the rest followed but one old long-faced hypocritical Baptist preacher, who said: "I will ask one question: do you believe in future punishments and rewards?" "I do, to some extent," answered I; "I accept Dr. Dick's definition of such things," and he said, "and who is Dr. Dick?" The reply was: "He is the most eminent theologian of the day, and all ministers of the gospel of any note quote him in their sermons." He got up and went out with his head and tail both down, which left Captain Jeff and the officer alone, and he was so nonplused that he did not speak for some time. Finally, Captain Jeff said: "I await your orders, sir," to which he said, "I don't know what to do; there have been so many hard reports to General Oaks against you that he sent me here to arrest you and some others, and to leave no leaf unturned to prove your guilt. If it was left to me, I would do as Christ did when the hypocrites brought the woman to Him to be rebuked. He said to them: 'He that is guiltless let him cast the first stone,' and they all sneaked off just as your accusers have done this evening." "When I gave them the opportunity to question you there was not one of them that had the courage to ask you a question but that old hypocritical preacher, and the question he asked had nothing whatever to do with your guilt or innocence." He finally said, "I suppose I will have to require you to give bond." "Draw up the bond and I will fill it."

The bond was drawn in the sum of one thousand dollars, if called for in thirty days; if not, then it was null and void. The bond was filled at once, Emanuel Sampson as surety, and our Captain Jeff was told that he could go in peace.

At six o'clock he mounted Mansfield; it was twelve miles to his home, but at seven o'clock he was siting in his home, his noble wife on one knee and his two lovely children on the other, again the happiest little family on the frontier of Texas.

The days came and went, and when the clock struck six on the evening of the thirtieth day and no call had been made for him, he walked up to his wife, threw his arms around her, pressed her to his heart with a fervent "thank God, my Mollie, we are free once more!" He had lost six years in defence of his country, his home and his fireside; his good stock of horses had been driven off by Big Foot and his band; his cattle was all gone but two cows, and summing everything up he found that he had to commence again almost at the bottom round of the ladder, but he had his noble wife and two lovely children, his good health and a determination to overcome every obstacle that might lie in his path.

He made rails, opened up more land, and as he was a good carpenter, all the neighbors that wanted work of that kind gave him the contracts in preference to any other, and gave him more than they could have got the same work done for, as they were sure of an honest job. As fast as he worked out money he invested it in cattle, and as cattle were very low in price, he soon had a nice bunch of cattle, and added to this all the men in the adjoining counties gave him full authority to use their cattle as he pleased. This enabled him to make contracts to put up herds of cattle for sale, and as his business rapidly increased he took a partner, G. C. Arnett, who had been in his company in the late war.

They drove beeves to New Orleans, and to the packeries at Calvert, Texas, and stock cattle to Kansas, and steadily invested their profits in the purchase of entire stocks of cattle, marks and brands. In a short time the firm controlled seventy marks and brands in the counties of Burnet, Lampasas, Llano and San Saba, and prosperity followed his every effort as he so richly deserved.

# CHAPTER VI.

**Capt. Jeff is Wrongfully Indited by the Civil Law, for which he Makes a Bad Break but Through the Christianizing Influence of the Noble Wife he Guards Himself Against Like Occurrances**

It has been said by some wise man "that every sweet has a bitter," and that unalloyed happiness and prosperity can only last an indefinite period of time, and such was the case with our Captain Jeff. Federal Judge, Federal Prosecuting Attorney and Sheriff were appointed for Burnet County and the twelve men that sat as jurors in Captain Jeff's quasi military court martial were appointed grand jurors and they found bills of indictment against Professor Holland, Captain Jeff and fifty-eight others for murder and robbery during the late war. So our hero's troubles commenced again just where they were left off.

The papers were served on Captain Jeff and sixteen others; they all easily gave bond for their appearance at court; they then employed a lawyer, the best that could be found, to fight their case, turned loose all their business and stood ready and waiting for the call of court. When it was called they were all in waiting, and the State put off the trial till the next term, and the next term was the same. When the third term came around they were all in waiting and anxious for trial, but the District Attorney was ordered by the Judge to throw the whole batch out of court, and so they were deprived of a tongue revenge, for their attorney was well prepared to show to the court and to the citizens of Burnet County the low down villainy of the grand jury in finding the bills worded as they were worded.

Here the pent-up feelings of Captain Jeff for that grand jury could not be restrained any longer, as he, with all the others had been deprived of their tongue revenge through their attorney. He determined to take revenge with his own strong arm, steady nerve and quick eye. He commenced to drink, the only bad generalship he ever displayed. His friends, all those that had been indicted with him, and many more crowded around him, got hold on him and by sheer force and persuasion got him out of town, and Jas. W. Taylor, whom he loved as a brother got him on his own horse and took him to Taylor's home and kept him till the next morning. Taylor sent to town, had his horse brought out and would not let him leave until he promised him that he would not go through town as he went home, and that he would never seek a difficulty with his persecutors, and he kept his promise with his true friend, J. W. Taylor.

# CHAPTER VII.

### His Wife's Little Tea Party.

A short time after this his wife gave a litle teaparty to some of her lady friends and on this occasion she opened a few bottles of her pure unfermented juice of the celebrated Mission grapes and her lady friends proposed that they all drink a toast, each one to select her own subject and insisted that the hostess lead off.

She filled her wine glass, rose to her feet, raised her arm to full length. The thoughts uppermost in her mind how a few days since Jeff came so near blasting his and her hopes of happiness through this life, she spoke and said: "Here is to my husband; may he never get tight, but tight or straight, my husband." The next one said: "Here is to our noble hostess; may her every wish be gratified, and may we live to emulate her courage, patience and womanly devotion," and all the others said: "Amen, amen, amen, amen."

Captain Jeff was away from home for a few days on some business when this little teaparty was given; before he returned he heard of it and the toast his wife had drank to him; when he got home he said: "Mollie, open a bottle of your grape juice; I want to drink to you a pledge that will relieve you of all dread or anxiety that called forth your toast." She quickly and joyously opened the bottle and set him a wine glass; he filled it to the brim, then raised his arm and said: "My Mollie, in this glass of the pure juice of the grape I pledge to you, God helping me, that from this time on that I will not make, sell or use as a beverage any spirituous or malt liquors; that wherever I go I will keep this pledge to you sacred." And in after years he made a tour of the entire State of California with the American Horticultural Society, as he was a member of that society. The society stopped over at a town called Fresno; the citizens came forward from every quarter with their best private conveyances to welcome them and drive them over the country and show them their fine orchards, vineyards and wineries.

The first visit was to the Barton vineyard of six hundred and forty acres, with winery attached, at which place they all halted and alighted and formed a procession of twos and marched into a long room where was spread a long table covered with snow white linen, wine glasses and all varieties of all the very finest wines that California could boast of. When they reached the table they filed right and left and moved forward to fill up the table.. When the lead man reached the table he faced about so as to overlook the table and all the guests. He said: "If there is any one present who will not taste any of this wine let him hold up his hand," and in an instant Captain Jeff's hand went up to the full length of his arm, and he held it there so all could see who it was. The spokesman at the head of the table said: "One hand up," and Captain Jeff slowly lowered his hand to its natural position, the honored hero of the occasion.

When the wine banquet was over, the ladies and one or two of the gentlemen who were strictly temperate, crowded around our Captain Jeff, heartily shaking his hand and complimenting him for his courage and devotion to principle so publicly explained.

They said: "We were not nor did not taste the wine, but we did not have the moral courage to follow your noble example. How could you do it?" "It was without any effort on my part; it struck my ear as a challenge to principle, and in an instant my principle accepted the challenge, and oh, my dear friends, I was rewarded for the act a thousand times more than my feble tongue can express." "Was the reward invisible to all but yourself?" "It was." "Will you then please give us an explanation?" "I will, and I will do so as fearless of criticism as I was when I held up my hand. The moment I held up my hand an angelic face appeared to me as if suspended in the air in front of me and a little higher than my head looking me straight in the eyes, and a heavenly radiance of approval beamed from its every feature, and in that moment my stature seemed to grow higher and higher and higher and the world seemed to be under my feet, and I lost sight of the audience, the table, wine and wine glasses, and I can only add that my feelings were not earthly, but heavenly."

The party was banqueted every day for thirty days in making the tour of California, and he left the State not knowing whether California wine was good or bad or indifferent, and he says that alcoholic liquors is the best tasted of anything that he ever tasted.

We hope the reader will pardon this digression. It seemed to be necessary in this connection to show up the firmness and devotion of the man of which we write.

# CHAPTER VIII.

**Richard Coke is Elected Governor. A Battallion of Rangers is Ordered. Captain Jeff is Commissioned and Raises a Company, Goes on Duty and Renews his Pursuit of the Big Foot Indian**

As they were making the tour of California, great changes were progressing in the great State of Texas. A State election had been held. Richard Coke was elected Governor, and Richard Hubard Lieutenant Governor, and a Democratic Legislature which passed a special act authorizing the raising of a battalion of Rangers, in which the opportunity will be offered for us to return to the thread of our narrative in the long pursuit and final capture and death of the noted Big Foot Kiowa chief and his lieutenant Jape, the barbarous and bloody Comanche.

As soon as it was known that the battalion of Rangers was to be organized Jas. W. Taylor at once got up two petitions and got them signed by all the leading men of Burnet County. One to Captain Jeff asking him to take the command of the battalion, and the other to Governor Coke asking him to appoint Captain Jeff to its command. Jas. W. Taylor went in person with the petition to Governor Coke, where he met Senator W. H. Westfall and solicited his assistance, which was the very thing that was uppermost in the Senator's mind in regard to the commander of the battalion, as he had been on many scouts after Indians with our whilom Captain.

Senator Westfall got General Shelly, an eminent lawyer, to draw up a petition and recommendation and got it signed by all the members of both houses of the Legislature and all the bankers and leading business men of Austin. But Governor Coke being the Democratic party of Texas, as Cleveland was the Democratic party of the United States, he gave the majorship to John B. Jones, a man that had no experience whatever in Indian warfare; a man that never lived on the frontier and was not identified with the frontier in any way. His only apology was that he knew John B. Jones and did not know our Captain Jeff, and that he intended to give the appointment to Jones from the start, regardless of fitness, for he was his personal friend and that he had seen his bravery tested many a time on the battle field in the Confederate war.

In conversation with Captain Jeff after the appointment, he said: "Captain Jeff, you have the best recommendation in my office for the command of the battalion that any man could have, and I have stepped over it, and I hope you and your people will not think hard of me for it.'" The reply was: "You are our Governor, and it is your bounden duty to render to all the people a just service as you may see it." The Governor then said: "Will you accept a commission as Captain of one of the campaigns?" The reply was: "Will the Governor give me three days to consider it?" He said: "Yes, as many days as you want." While waiting for the expiration of the three days to give the Governor his final decision he received a letter from his wife saying: "Jeff, do come home as soon as you can; that Big Foot brute of an Indian that murdered poor Mrs. Johnson and her dear little innocent children almost at our very door has just been here in the neighborhood, and I am almost frightened to death for fear that he will come and kill me and the children or some other good family."

When he had finished reading his wife's letter, his mind was made up that here was another chance open for him to rid the frontier of this dread curse that hung over them like a pall both day and night. He folded his wife's letter, put it in his breast pocket, and started at once for the Governor's office.

On his way he met James Cornell, a man that had seen and done much service on the frontier and was one of his particular friends.

He said: "Jim, I am going to the Governor's office to accept a Captain's commission in the frontier battalion. Won't you go in with me as my first lieutenant?" He said: "I can't get the appointment." "Come with me, and we will see." They went together to the Governor's office, and Captain Jeff introduced Cornell to him and said: "Governor, if you will give me Mr. Cornell here, as my First Lieutenant, I will accept the Captaincy in the Frontier Battalion, for, Governor, if I accept a Captaincy, there will be a great deal expected of me." The Governor replied: "Yes, more than any man in the battalion." Here the opportunity was presented to give the Governor a little thrust and the Captain said: "Governor, you ought to except the Major." The Governor winced, for he felt that the point was well taken; however he said: "Hold on here, a few minutes while I go and talk to Adjutant General Steel about your First Lieutenant."

In a few moments the Governor returned and said: "You may have Mr. Cornell for your First Lieutenant, and you are the only Captain that will be shown that courtesy after being sworn into the service."

The Adjutant General turned over to Captain Jeff a pair of mules and hack, loaded the hack with arms and ammunition, and ordered him to go and raise a company of seventy-five men, and to swear them into service, and to furnish them all the necessary supplies and to go on duty at once. As the country was overrun with Indians and outlaws, Captain Jeff and his Lieutenant started at once with the arms and ammunition to raise a select company of men and horses with all possible dispatch.

When they got near the Captain's home, they saw a man coming meeting them riding a fine iron gray horse. The Captain said: "Jim, if I did not know that old Selum was dead, I would say that man was riding him; he has his every movement, and I am going to buy him, if he can be bought, for something tells me that that is the horse that is to run down my Big Foot adversary that has been so fortunate as to outgeneral me so many times." By the time this conversation was ended, the parties met, and after the usual salutations the following conversation was had:

"Mister, how old is your horse?" "Six years old." "What stock is he?" "The best four mile stock that is raised in Arkansas; he has never been beaten on the track." "Is he gentle?" "Yes, gentle as a dog, and as brave as a lion." "Well, that is the very horse I am looking for; I once owned a horse that was a dead match to yours, but I think my horse was the better horse of the two."

He said: "Stranger, that horse don't live that is a better horse than this, my horse, Selum." "Is that his name?" "Yes, he was named after the horse that young Scotch McDonell rode in the Revolutionary War in General Marion's company." "Well, that was my horse's name, too, and he was named after the same horse of Revolutionary fame." "Well, what will you take for him?" "I am a new comer here, and I will need a good work team, and if you will give me a pair of good horses and one hundred dollars in cash, you may have him." Without any hesitation, the Captain replied: "It is a trade; it is only one mile to my house; come with us and I will fix you up with a good team and one hundred dollars cash."

After reaching the Captain's house it only required a few minutes to make a final close of the trade, and he mounted one of the horses and rode off saying, "Good-bye, gentlemen, and good-bye, Selum." When he was gone, the Captain hollowed: "Oh, Mollie! Come out here." After introducing her to Lieutenant Cornell, he said: "Mollie, do you know that horse?" She looked at him, in perfect amazement, and finally stammered out: "Y-yes, n-no; if I didn't know that old Selum was dead, that the Indians killed him, and you on him, and that you carried your saddle home on your back, I would say, yes, I know him, that he was Selum." "Well, Mollie, he is Selum number two, and I have a commission in my pocket to raise seventy-five men and go Rangering, and I bought Selum number two to ride." She exclaimed: "Why, Jeff, you have been a soldier and worse than a soldier for the eight years, and I have been a kind of a grass widow all that time." "Say, Mollie, what is a grass widow?" "It's a woman that her husband goes off and leaves her all the time." "Then what is a kind of a grass widow?" "It's a woman that her husband goes off and leaves her most of the time; and when I married you, I thought I was going to have a husband all the time." He replied: "Then I have been only a sort of a husband a very little of the time."

"Mollie, you say, and correctly, that I have been a soldier for eight years; did you know that No. 9 was my lucky number? My mother was born in the year 1809, you were born in 1839 and you two are the greatest women I have ever known, and that I was born in 1829, that our boy Jeff was born in 1859, and circumstances, it seems, over which I have no control cause me to accept a soldier's life one more year, which makes that No. 9. Why, Mollie, I used to play poker before I was overshadowed by your Christianizing influence, and whenever I got a pair of nines I always staid in the Jack pot, and if I got the third one in the draw I never laid them down."

"Oh, pshaw, Jeff, what do I know about such talk as Jack pot. stay in and lay down, three nine, and so on? But if your destiny was or is to soldier nine years, I hope kind Providence will protect you in your lucky No. 9, as it seems to have protected you for the last eight." "Mollie, let me say to you, don't have any fears for my personal safety, for that small voice that has protected me through all my life tells me to go, and that I will be successful, and that when the full time alloted to me as a soldier has expired that I will return to you and the children victorious, mounted on Selum and in the best of health, and will find you and the children well and happy; then I will lay aside my arms of death to man and try and practice war no more." She said: "God grant it; amen."

Lieutenant Cornell remained at Captain Jeff's that night and in the morning the Captain told him to go right on to Brownwood, Brown County, where he had lived for years and knew every man in the county, and to pick twenty-five men and horses, the very best that he could select; then the Orderly Sergeant and one duty Sergeant, and you go on to Camp Colorado and tell Lieutenant Best that I send the same order to him that I give to you. He can select one Duty Sergeant and two Corporals. I will pick twenty-five men here in Burnet County and select one Commissary Sergeant, two Duty Sergeans and two Corporals, and rendezvous at Brownwood. Expedite matters as fast as you can, having an eye single to the good of the service." By this mode of wise procedure in a very short time a company of seventy-five men was raised, giving the counties of Burnet, Brown and Coleman an equal devision of commissioned and non-commissioned officers and men.

In the short space of two weeks the company was rendezvoused at Brownwood, formed into line, and the Captain administered the oath necessary in military organizations, the muster roll made out, the non-commissioned officers appointed as agreed upon, a contract made with John T. Gilber, a merchant of Brownwood, to furnish supplies, and the company went on duty at once. And the Major commanding and the Quartermaster and Battalion Doctor publicly said that it was the best company in the battalion, or that could be raised in the State, and that Captain Jeff was the only man that could command them. And this was no flattery either, for they had been selected for health, strength, horsemanship and experts with the lasso, and a perfect familiarity of frontier life, and like Davy Crockett of old, they were half horse and half aligator, many of them standing six feet two inches in physique, perfect fac similes of the Big Foot Indian of which we write, less the foot. The Captain turned over a posse of his men to the Sheriff of Brown County and they soon arrested or drove out all the lawless characters, John Wesley Harden among the rest, while he turned his particular attention to scouting for Indians.

The trails of his scouting party could be seen in every direction which kept the Indians from making their monthly raids, which gave the settlers such encouragement that they wrote back to their friends in the other States to come; that they had the very best of protection, which gave impetus to immigration, and Brown and adjoining counties rapidly filled up with first-class people, which greatly assisted in driving back the Indians.

# CHAPTER IX.

Sergeant Andrew Mather is Sent on a Scout into Callahan Co., Camps Near Caddo Peak. John Parsons is Sent out to Kill a Deer for Meat, Encounters Big Foot and Band, Makes His Celebrated Shot and Big Foot Dodges the Bullet and Makes another one of his Providential Escapes.

One of the first scouts made by Captain Jeff's company was commanded by Sergeant Andrew Mather, further mention of which will be made as our recital progresses. He was ordered to take fifteen men and make a scout through the roughs of Callahan County near the Caddo Peaks, etc. The second evening after starting he struck camp near West Caddo Peak, and as it was not customary for this company to carry more than meat enough for one day when going on a scout, this scout was no exception to the general rule, so on camping, Sergeant Mather ordered John Parsons, who was a fine shot, and an experienced hunter, to take his gun and go out and kill a deer for supper, saying: "If you find a bunch of cattle don't shoot; come back to camp and we will go and rope one, as you know the Captain's orders are not to shoot at anything but Indians, not even the Devil himself, if it can possibly be avoided, and I think too much of old Captain Jeff to break one of his orders." So saying, Parsons slung his gun over his shoulder and mached off. He had not been gone but about five or ten minutes when they heard his gun fire, and he hollowing for life, saying: "Come on, boys! Come on! Here are the damn rascals! Come on!"

Mather hollowed: "Saddle your horses, boys, quick! quick!" and in less time than it takes to write about it, the horses were saddled. By this time Parsons had got to camp, and he fell exhausted for want of breath. Mather said: "Parsons, did you kill a deer?" When he had regained his breath sufficiently to speak, he said: "I did not, but I killed a —— —— Indian." It is to be hoped that this rough expression may be pardonable under the very exciting circumstances. Here we will let Parsons tell his own story in as few words as possible before going to verify his statement. He said:

"I was walking along slowly looking for cattle or deer and when I saw horses' legs coming towards me the limbs of the trees came down so low that I could not see the horses' bodies. I squatted down and when they got in sixty or seventy yards of me I saw that old Big Foot was in the lead; in an instant I thought my only chance for life was to kill him and the one just behind him, and I tried to say, 'Now, Parsons, make the best shot of your life,' so I aimed and pulled the trigger, and I'll be d—n if old Big Foot didn't dodge the bullet and I killed the one behind him! He fell forward, grabbed both arms around his horses' neck, then I run and hollowed for life."

While Parsons was telling his story some of the boys were saddling his horse, so then they all mounted and went in haste to verify Parson's statement.

When they reached the spot, the mystery of Big Foot dodging the bullet of Parson's gun was fully explained, for just at the moment that Parsons pulled the trigger Big Foot's horse stepped into a hole made by some little animal, that burrows in the ground. He fell forward and came below Parson's sight thus dodging the bullet. Reader, was this luck again for Big Foot, or what? Parsons' identity of Big Foot was correct, for there plainly to be seen was his tracks where he jumped off his fallen horse and ran to the assistance of one of his falling braves. From the amount of blood at the spot, Parsons' shot must have been fatal.

The trail was taken with as much dispatch as possible, and in less than a mile they reached the hard, stony and bushy hills just north of the Peak, where it was impossible for them to follow the trail any further. Go on, Big Foot, go on, there is a man on your trail! It has been "diamond cut diamond" with you for several years, but the time will come sooner or later, when your diamond will cease to sparkle, and its brilliancy will go out forever in this world.

Sergeant Mather's scout returned without seeing or hearing of any more Indians. The next light moon the Captain sent out Lieut. Best on a scout; he camped on the Jim Ned, above Old Camp Colorado. After supper the horses were all picketed out, and the guards properly stationed; the men lay down, and some of them had gone to sleep, when the Indians slipped up around the camp and fired into it, yelling like demons. Lieut. Best sprang to his feet and hollowed to every man to get to his horse quick, quick. He ran barefooted to his horse, and all the men followed his example, taking their arms with them. Each one when he got to his horse began firing as rapidly as he could in the direction from which the yells and firing of the Indians came, which soon stopped the yelling and firing, and in half an hour the camp was again still and quiet. On examination the only casualty was one horse killed, which was seen to fall at the first volley that the Indians fired. This small loss was lucky, for the arrows and bullets flew thick and fast at the first onslaught.

This made another one of Big Foot's lucky escapes. As the Indians had been driven off nothing more could be done but to double the guards and stand their ground until morning. On examination of the surroundings of the camp it was demonstrated that this attack was made by Big Foot and his band, for the difference in the size of his tracks and the others proved it to be he without any doubt. The Indians had tied their horses some distance from the camp and made the attack on foot, and when their attack was met with such cool and determined resistance they ran back to their horses, mounted them and rode off in different directions, one of Big Foot's tactics, and a sure one too, to prevent being trailed or followed, for it is almost impossible to trail one horse any distance, while a bunch can be trailed with all ease.

Lieut. Best rode in a big circle, but could not find where the Indians came together, consequently he returned to camp without anything else to report.

## CHAPTER X.

Lieutenant Best is Sent on a Scout. Camps on Jim Ned and is Attacked After Night by Big Foot and Band. Cool Bravery and Discipline Whipped Him off With Only the Loss of One Horse, Shot Through the Heart.

The next light moon Major Jones made his monthly visit of inspection and called on the Captain to take scouts and go with him to Fort Concho. They rode very hard, and when near Fort Concho the Major told the Captain that he could go back and make a scout on his return, and that he would go on to Fort Concho with the men he had with him.

They were then in a spot where there was but little grass, but remembered passing over good grass some ten miles back, and were compelled to ride back to get feed for their horses.

The spot of grass was reached after dark, the horses were all side lined and turned loose to grass, two men to guard them.

The others built fires and got supper, but before they had time to eat it the Indians, twenty or twenty-five in number, made a desperate and reckless charge into and through the camp, firing guns, pistols and arrows, knocking the fires and supper helter skelter, and yelling like demons.

They stampeded all the horses, and drove them much faster than the men could run, but the men ran and fired after them as long as the sound of the horses' feet could be heard.

When they were completely exhausted, they stopped and sat down, some cursing and swearing, and some laughing at the figure they would cut walking forty miles carrying their saddles, etc.

When they all had had their say, Captain Jeff said: "This is pretty tough on old Jeff's brag company, to go on a scout and be so badly outgeneraled by old Big Foot that we all have to walk forty miles to camp carrying our saddles, but let me show you how much worse it could have been. You see how all of us missed being killed or wounded; think it over, and you will say that was almost if not a miracle. See, we are all unhurt, and will if possible be more determined to get even with our Big Foot friend (?), for this will encourage him to hunt for us to get some more of our good horses.

The State will pay for your horses and as for me, old Selum will be back here before morning, for the Indian that cuts his side lines and mounts him will be a dead or crippled Indian if there are any trees near this place, for the horse will run away with him and throw him against a tree or my name is not Jeff. Boys, you won't have to walk to camp; old Selum will carry me to camp long before night tomorrow, and I will send back horses for you to ride on; old Jeff's boys are horse soldiers, not foot soldiers." When this last talk was finished a distant rumbling like horses' feet was heard. The boys sprang to their feet, some thinking the Indians were coming back. As the sounds came nearer and clearer old Jeff bursted out in a laugh as the sound, tone and beat of that hoof was indelibly impressed on his ear and nerve. When the running horse came near enough to hear the Captain hollowed at the top of his voice: "Selum! Selum! My boy. Here, here!" A sharp, keen neigh of recognition was heard in answer and Selum dashed up to where the men stood. The Captain said in a gentle tone, "Selum, my boy, come here," and the noble horse walked up to him and put his head over his shoulder, with a gentle whinny. The Captain then said, "Boys, what did I tell you? See this rawhide tug tied around Selum's under jaw?. Why, an Indian could no more ride this horse with that tug than I could fly like an eagle, or knock down a mountain with my fist!"

The boys said: "We know that there is not a man in your company that can or ever will ride Selum without his running away, but yourself, and we think that he has made up his mind that no other man shall ride him." They trudged on back to the temporary camp feeling very much like foot soldiers for the time being.

Captain Jeff mounted Selum and said, "Boys, while away the time as best you can until tomorrow night, and you will be rangers again, and I will have you back in camp in three days."

He rode off, and at four o'clock he was at his headquarters camp and reported his defeat. The next morning he started back sixteen men with sixteen lead horses and in three days he had all of his men at headquarters camp. At roll call that evening, the orderly sergeant reported all men present, sixteen horses absent without leave. "Charge them up to bad generalship of the Captain, and good generalship of the Big Foot ingin."

Sixteen other good horses were purchased and the company was soon again in good shape for duty.

# CHAPTER XI.

**High Water, Discipline and the Ranger Feast.**

In the month of August Major Jones made his regular return visit all along the line, and on leaving Camp Company "E" he ordered Captain Jeff to take a detachment of men and go down on Muke Water and buy a crop of corn that was reported to be growing on that stream; so immediately after the Major's departure, the captain took three men and went at once to carry out the Major's orders. It was raining a slow rain at the time they started, and it rained steadily and slowly all the day and night.

The corn was purchased and the little party camped in an old schoolhouse, and stood the regular guard (as guard was never omitted with this company, under any circumstances) the Captain always taking his regular turn on occasions like this where the scout or expedition was few in number.

The next morning it was still raining the steady, slow rain, that had been falling for eighteen hours. After a hastily prepared breakfast, the captain orderel "Boots and Saddles" as this company never stopped for any thing when duty called.

Their course was up Muke Water stream, which was now swollen to a rushing torrent, and covered the entire valley from hill to hill.

The Captain rode his favorite horse that had always been equal to any emergency, and as they were all wet to the skin, he thought to try his boys' luck in water as well as on dry land; so he turned Selum directly to the road that led up the creek valley which was completely covered with driftwood and water from three to ten feet deep where the small depressions run into the main channel.

At every plunge the boys cheered and hollowed: "Where old Jeff dares to go, we can follow.' This headlong and reckless ride was kept up for some ten miles to where the road leading from headquarters camp to Brownwood crossed the Muke Water stream.

Here the Captain found his company wagon and harness washed up and lodged against a large mesquite tree, and heard at the same time a yell from the adjacent hill, and on going to reconnoiter, he found two of his men that had been sent to Brownwood the evening before by the commisary sergeant for supplies. They had camped for the night near the creek. They saved their lives by swimming and left the wagon to its fate.

Here the captain and his little party halted to assist his men and wagon to cross the stream at the earliest moment possible. About three o'clock that evening two men from headquarters camp rode up and reported to the Captain that the entire camp was washed away; that one man and six horses were drowned, and that there was not a vestige of anything left in the camp, only the men, most of them with only their night clothes, but each and every man had all his arms and cartridge belt, but no other subsistance but air and muddy water. So much for discipline. This company could not be taken by surrprise in the loss of arms for immediate use only by a destructive flash of lightning. Let us briefly explain: The horses were all tied to a picket line, and a sentinel walked the line every night as regular as the tick of the clock.

The sentinel discovered a roll of water several feet high rolling down the entire valley of Home Creek in which the camp was located in a beautiful grove of spreading elm trees. He (the sentinel) gave the alarm with might and main, to cut the horses loose; every man sprang up, grabbed his arms and ran to the picket line to cut his horse loose, and by the time that was done they had to get to trees as best they could, and sit perched upon limbs, and shiver with the cold, as there was nothing they could do until the water subsided from under the trees; after which they climbed down, and two of the men went to the hills and got the horses that were not drowned. They plunged into the raging torrent to carry the news of their terrible dilema, and pressing necessities, to the Captain. This was one of the most daring feats performed by any two single men in the Company. Their names, as well as remembered, were Curley Hacher and Josephes Rush.

He at once sent them back to the camp with orders to Lieut Best to get a conveyance and send escort with the drowned man to Camp Colorado and to have him buried with the honors of war. The others to kill and barbecue a beef and subsist as best they could until he could get to them with rations. The necessities of the situation required heroic exertions. He at once mounted his horse bareback, rode to the stream and plunged in to see if it was possible to cross with the wagon. The current was so strong that it bore him and the horse much farther down than he expected, and it was with great exertions that his horse mounted to firm footing on the other bank. After resting his horse, he went up higher above the ford, and his horse landed him safely back at the ford. As there was no possible chance to get the wagon across he had to sit down and chew the cud of anxiety until the water fell to a crossing depth. At nine or ten o'clock that night the water had fallen to such an extent that the Captain ordered the horses hitched up saying, "Boys, we will plunge that creek at all hazards; our boys in camp are looking to us for grub and they shall have it. Tie the wagon bed fast to the axles," which was done, and they moved forward to the bank of the creek; here he placed two of his men to cross below the team, the other above the team. He went in the lead, saying, "Now come, and give them mules the biggest scare you can; that is, make them jump across, or as far out as possible. If we get across quick enough, the current won't capsize the wagon." The plunge was made as directed, and the landing was well made, and when the top of the bank was reached. he Ranger yell of victory could have been heard for miles around.

Turning to the driver, the Captain said: "John, we want all there is in them mules; keep up with us; when they fail, we will tie on to the end of the tongue with our ropes, and pull the wagon at the horns of our saddles" In this way, double-quick time was made to Brownwood, and they plunged into swimming water inside of the town, but they made a successful crossing, loaded the wagon with grub as the first essential, and were on the road back to the camp before daylight. In leaving Brownwood, they went around the water that they swam on going in, and when they got to Muke Water creek it had fallen to a fordable depth.

By urging the animals to their utmost, camp was reached by one o'clock that day, and as the relief party drove into camp a shout of joy rent the air that will ever be remembered by all the participants. A beef had been killed, the hide washed and hung up to drip ready to kneed the flour, a sack of which was emptied on the hide, a bountiful quantity of the inside fat was cut fine; salt, soda, fat and flour were well mixed, and four men went to work with a will urged on by the cravings of hunger, and in less than it takes to write it the dough was well kneaded, and each man came with his stick for his allowance.

A bountiful fire had been made in anticipation of this pleasant event, and the beef was cooking to a finish. Reader, let your imagination picture this scene around this fire. Each man cooking his bread a la Ranger style. The beef was now cooked to a finish, and here the most enjoyable feast that was ever eaten was enjoyed by Company "E," Texas Rangers, Frontier Battalion.

After the feast was over orders were given to all to spread out down the valley and collect everything that had been caught in brush and driftwood, and most of the camp equippage was recovered, but badly disfigured by its terrible encounter with a second Noah's flood, only the equippage didn't have a Mt. Ararat to lodge upon. Everything that could be found was gathered and the camp was moved to Mud Creek and remained there until the reductions of the battalion was made.

Thos. Clark who is now a successful merchant in the prosperous and thriving town of Abilene, Texas, was at that time the youngest member of the Company. For his sterling worth and honor to report marks and brands correctly, and his ability to kill beef, he was appointed by the Captain to that position while in camp or on scouts.

# CHAPTER XII.

Sargeant Mather is Sent on Scout in Runnels County in which Discipline Coupled with Individual Bravery Kills the Largest Bear in West Texas, with a Bowie Knife.

After the new camp was properly arranged Sergeant Mather was ordered to take twenty men and go out on a scout in which the discipline of this company is further demonstrated.

It was standing orders while on a scout that the men were not allowed to shoot at any thing but an Indian, and when it was necessary to get meat the commander of the scout should detail one or two men to get the meat while all the others remained on duty. In this instance, the scout was marching regularly along, when one of the largest (if not the largest) bears that ever was seen in Texas, came marching slowly along, as if to banter them to shoot and break their orders. He came nearer and nearer, and when he had got within sixty or seventy yards of the scout Sergeant Mather said, "Halt, boys, remain in your positions," and quickly taking down his small, nice rawhide lariat, he dashed after the bear and before he ran one hundred yards he threw his rope and it tightened around the bear's neck. The bear grabbed the rope in his mouth to bite it in two. Mather sprang off his horse; the horse was trained to hold anything that the lasso was thrown over. Mather drew his Bowie knife, ran to the bear, and drove it through his heart before he could bite the lariat in two. The other men remained as they were ordered, all except one— Bill Dunman, who ran to Mather for fear that the bear would get him tangled up in the rope.

The bear's hide was brought into camp, was stretched and hung up with but one hole in it. The rope was hung up by the hide with the marks of the bear's teeth on it as proof of bravery and discipline. This scout returned to camp without seeing any sign of Indians. This company didn't keep its headquarters camp more than two months in one place, and in moving always selected a camp so there was a mountain in four or five miles of it, so that a plain view of the surrounding country could be had with good field glasses for miles around. The Captain selected at the start four men for spies that had no other duty to perform. Early each morning two of them would mount their horses and go to the spy mountain and remain on duty until after dinner when they would be relieved by the other two, and this spy duty was strictly kept up every day unless it rained all day.

At this time the headquarters camp was on Mud Creek in Coleman County, in heavy post oak timber. About one half mile west of the camp was a beautiful mountain for spy purposes, and the camp could not be seen from its base. The spies had been kept on it for nearly two months when it commenced to rain one morning before·the time for the spies to go on duty, and it rained all day until late in the evening so the spies were not sent out. Bill Sinclare's horses would always graze off up to the spy mountain whenever he was turned lose, but there was no fear of losing him by Indians as the spies stood guard there all day and every day. Late in the evening of this day Sinclaire went out to the mountain to get his horse, and lo and behold! there between the camp and the mountain was an Indian trail of seventeen horses.

Sinclare's horse was hobbled, and just in the right place for them to take him along. Sinclare made 2:40 time in going back to camp with the report. Orders were at once given for seventeen men to saddle their horses and in five minutes the scout started; they went out to the mountain and took the trail, Mexican Joe as trailer, as he had been enlisted for that purpose, and could trail almost equal to a bloodhound.

The ground was wet, and the trail was followed at a brisk lope for about twenty miles, where the Indians had halted within about one hundred yards of a man's house and in all probability were intending to murder the family, but before they had time to carry that into effect, the Rangers came in sight.

The Rangers did not check their horses, but charged right onto them. The Indians were so taken by surprise, that they were almost panic stricken. At the first volley of the Rangers one Indian fell dead and two more were wounded. Sinclare's horses fell dead and the bow of the Indian that rode him was shot in two so the Indian had no other arms but a butcher knife; this he drew and bending down his head he dashed into the Rangers, uttering the wild shrieks of an enraged bull. He made one desperate lunge at Sergeant Mather with his knife and would have killed him, but Mather was the best horseman in the company, and just as the knife descended he threw himself to the opposite side of his horse, Wallace, who received the blow that was intended for his rider.

The knife was driven through the saddle blanket and into Wallace's shoulderblade. At that instant the brave, devoted and heroic Indian fell with four army six shooter balls driven through the vital part of his body. As a deed of bravery, devotion and heroism it was never surpassed, no, not by Arnold Winkelried. His devotion to his chief and his comrades caused him to give his life to give them a chance to get away, for when he had made his mad charge, uttering the shrieks of an enraged bull all eyes were turned on him, and by the time he fell all the others were out of sight and gone, as it was dark, and the timber and brush was thick at the place. As nothing further could be done in the darkness, and it was only six miles to the town of Brownwood the Captain took his men to Brownwood where accommodations could be had for men and horses. After reaching Brownwood, the men were bountifully fed at the hotels, horses all well cared for at the livery stables, all but the Captain's norse, he was put in a private stable, and the next morning the door was open, and the Captain's horse was gone. This was very annoying to the Captain as he was making all possible haste to go out to where the fight took place as he was anxious to take the trail of the Indians.

Two of the citizens of Brownwood, John McMahan and Henry Warmick were going out to where the fight took place to bring the dead Indians in for the people to see them, but as good luck would have it in this instance, the orderely sergeant had been sent into Brownwood two days before on some company business and he rode a number one horse, a race horse, that ran away with the sergeant every time the company went on drill. So the Captain called on the sergeant for his horse, which was cheerfully given, the captain saying: "Sergeant, my horse will be back here in the camp before night, if the Indians don't kill him, for they can't ride him."

The sergeant said, "No, the horse that can run away with Sergeant Mather, can run away with any Indian, even old Big Foot himself." The scout was mounted, and waiting for the Captain, as it took some little time for him to get the Sergeant's horse saddled. He said, "Sergeant Mather, Sergeant Arnet, Albert Arnet, Dr. King and Mexican Joe will remain with me; Lieut. Best, you go on with the balance of the men and we will overtake you before you get there. McMahan and Warmick remained with the Captain who soon started on behind the scout in a road that led to where the fight took place. The Captain's party had not gone more than a mile from Brownwood; he was riding in the lead when he discovered a fresh trail of horses near the road.

He at once turned his horse to it to investigate it, all the others of his little party followed him; they had not followed it but a short distance until they were fully convinced that it was Indians that had returned to Brownwood in the night and stolen fresh horses, the Captain's among the number. Here the Captain called for Mexican Joe to take the trail, and the race for life began. The Captain said, "Sergeant Mather, Wallace is disabled and can't stand the run, so you had better go and join Lieut. Best," to which the sergeant replied, "Wallace can stand anything, at any rate he will have to go until he falls," and drawing his quirt, he hit him a keen lick in the flank and drove him to the front just behind the trailer. Here Albert Arnet closed up by the side of Mather and in this manner the race was kept up until Joe's horse gave out. Here Mather and Arnet quickly dismounted and threw off their saddles, coats, hats, and the

Captain threw off his coat and they mounted their horses bareback, and took the trail side by side, and in a short distance Mather's horse ran against the limb of a tree and knocked him off. The Captain said, "Andrew, are you hurt?" He answered, "No," and the captain passed him, and in less than a hundred yards a limb struck the Captain, knocking him off. Mather came up and said, "Captain, are you hurt?" The Captain answered "No." "Then we are even," said Mather.

Just here a fine pair of U. S. red blankets were left hanging on a projecting limb, a little further on was two Indian saddles and bridles left on the trail, and everything they carried was thrown down to lighten their load. Just here the Indians were passing near the Ranger Camp and the Captain had completely run down the Sergeant's horse. He said, "Boys, they will go through Santa Anna Gap. Keep on after them, and I will go by the camp and get a fresh horse and meet you in the Gap."

When he reached the Gap his men had just passed through and Mather was standing by his noble horse, Wallace, coatless, hatless, and with his face all bloody from the limbs sticking in it, an object of disappointment and terror.

The Captain on his fresh horse soon overtook all that was left of his little party, to-wit: Sergeant Arnet, Albert Arnet and Dr. King, he himself making four, but they dauntlessly followed on to Robinson's Peak in Coleman County, where the country is very rough and brushy, here the Indians scattered, and their trail could not be followed any further. They had made the run from where the trail was first struck to Robinson's Peak, a distance of sixty miles, in seven hours.

The party killed a calf for meat, and wearily dragged themselves back to camp which they reached the next day sorely and sadly disappointed, for Big Foot's guiding spirit had carried him safely through another series of close places.

The first thing that greeted the Captain's eye when he returned to camp was Selum, standing where he was fed. The Captain dismounted and went directly to him, and patting him on the neck said, "Selum, my boy, did you bust another ingin?" to which he uttered his low familiar whinny, as much as to say, "you bet I did." The orderly sergeant coming up to greet the Captain said, "Selum did as you said he would, probably killed another Indian, and came back to Brownwood." "Did you ride him to camp?" "No, sir, I borrowed a horse and led him." The Captain then said, "I expect I have killed your horse, and if so, I will get you as good a one if he can be found." The sergeant replied, "I bought him to run Indians, and if you have killed him in that capacity, then he is well paid for," and this was the kind of men that composed Captain Jeff's company; nothing small about them but their feet. The scouting was kept up, but no more signs of Indians during this moon nor until near the full of the next moon

# CHAPTER XIII.

**Captain Jeff's Lucky No. "9" and the Promptings of the Still Small Voice Fully Verified.**

Lieut. Best was sitting in the camp tent one night and the subject came up of lucky numbers. The Captain said: "Lieutenant, have you a lucky number, and if so, what is it?" The Lieutenant said, "Yes, my lucky number all through life begins and ends with the figure nine. My mother was born on December 9, 1829, I was born on November 9, 1849, my wife was born on May 9, 1859, when all the flowers were in bloom, and she is the sweetest and loveliest rose that ever bloomed, and Rose is her name." Well, Lieutenant, the births of our family are coincidental all the way through, beginning or ending with the figure nine, and as tomorrow is the ninth of the month, I propose that we make a scout with nine men all told, including ourselves, and start precisely at nine o'clock a. m. I will select four of the men and you can select three;

1 select Sergeant Mather, Corporal Sackett, Bill Williams and Mexican Joe, for trailer." The Lieutenant then said: "I select Sergeant Arnet, Corporal Henry and Bill Dunman," so the names of the scout stood as follows:

1st—Captain Jeff, 2nd—Liuet. Best, 3rd—Sergeant Mather, 4th —Corporal Sackett, 5th—Bill Williams, 6th—Mexican Joe, 7th— Sergeant Arnett, 8th—Coropral Henry, 9th—Bill Dunman.

The list was made out and the Captain instructed the Lieutenant to notify the men to be in readiness to start at the appointed time, so at nine o'clock the following morning everything was in perfect readiness and the scout started at nine o'clock sharp. About three miles west of the headquarters camp was a Pass that the Indians sometimes went through as they returned from the settlements with their stolen horses, to which point the scout was directed at the start.

When they got near the Pass they saw a lone horseman sitting on his horse and they rode directly to him, and when near enough to recognize him the lone horseman hollowed "Hello! Captain! You are the very man of all men that I wanted to see at this time." The Captain replied, "Well, Jim, I am glad that I can be of service to you; what is wanted?" "The Indians, old Big Foot and band, stole a lot of horses yesterday in San Saba County near my place and my race horse, Gray Eagle, with the rest. I at once mounted this pony and took the trail with the hope that I might meet you or have a chance to send you word. I rode the trail hard all day yesterday and did not see anyone; when dark came on so that I couldn't see the trail I staked out my pony and laid down, and this morning followed it up to this pass. I don't think they are so far ahead but that you can overtake them before dark, but my horse Gray Eagle is good and gone from Jim Brown and his heirs forever, for there is not a horse on this frontier that can catch him." The Captain then said, "Jim, what distance does he run?" He replied: "One-half mile," to which the Captain smilingly said (patting Selum on the neck), "Jim, if that is Gray Eagle's distance, Selum can run over him or pull his head off with a hundred foot lariat in one mile and carry my weight, at which he laughed quizically. "Very well, the proof of the pudding is in the eating, and I feel that this is the day that I am to sample it after so many trials, and to fully test your opinion of the speed of Gray Eagle." He then said, "Boys, if we are to catch those Indians we can't stand here and talk race horse any longer, but get right down to business.

Jim Brown then said: "My pony can't go much farther, and it is no use for me to start on with you. I wish I had a good horse," to which the captain said, "and if you did, we would send you back, not that we doubt your bravery, for you have fully demonstrated by following and camping on the trail all alone that you could be depended on; we have made this a special scout of nine men and we do not want any more." "Then the captain said, "Joe, take the trail and make this the best effort of your life," which he did, keeping in a brisk trot or lope the entire day, with the exception of a short halt at three o'clock to eat a hasty lunch, and to rest and graze the horses for the onward pursuit.

At four o'clock they were again in the saddles and the same speed was kept up until it was growing dark, when they reached the summit of an elevation, and Joe came to a sudden halt and pointed towards where plainly to be seen was the Indians' fire, some two miles ahead under some large spreading elms on the bank of Valley Creek, in Runnels County.

Here a short consultation was held and they moved forward in a slow, steady walk in single file, Captain Jeff in the lead.

As they approached nearer the ground became sandy and their horses' feet made but very little noise. In this cautious manner they rode up behind a clump of small trees and brush and to within two hundred yards of the fire, where they halted and made a careful survey of the camp. They discovered that horses were tied north of the fire, that two horses were tied south of the fire, and that one horse was tied west of the fire and that their position was east of the fire. The Indians that rode the horses that were tied south of the fire and the one that rode the one tied west of the fire seemed to be on guard, as they walked about to the fire and back to the horses, and their movements indicated that they were placed on watch, and the horse that was west of the fire was from every appearance Jim Brown's race horse, Gray Eagle, and his rider was a woman. The other five Indians were busy around the fire cooking beef which they had killed when they made the halt. There were others out attending to the horses that they had ridden through the day. All the horses that were tied around the fire were fresh horses for the Indians to get away on in case they were overtaken. As they were so busy cooking, our party saw that plenty of time was given them to mature their plan of attack. It was plain to be seen from his size that Big Foot's horse was south of the fire and in all probability his lieutenant's also, as they two, with the women, were on guard as their every movement indicated.

Captain Jeff, speaking in a low tone said, "Corporal Sackett, you stay with me, I will take Big Foot and you take his lieutenant, and then we will capture the squaw. Lieutenant, you take all the other men and take everything at the fire and north of the fire, and when we start, don't hollow, let's get right out; then before they know it, and now go." And the charge was sudden and desperate in strict keeping with the Texas Ranger.

Let us follow Captain Jeff and Corporal Henry Sackett while they charge south of the fire after their select game, while Lieut. Best with the others charge north of the fire. At the sound of the horses' feet Big Foot and his lieutenant sprang to their horses, but before Big Foot could mount, Captain Jeff's six shooter spoke its voice of death and Big Foot's horse fell dead. Big Foot then turned and aimed his Spencer rifle, but before he could pull the trigger Captain Jeff's pistol spoke again and it's leaden messenger of death went to the mark knocking the hammer off of the Indian's gun and driving it into his cheek, then glanced down striking him in the jugular vein and breaking his neck. The blood spurted high and Big Foot fell to rise no more. His career of crime ended, and the warnings of the still small voice were verified.

Just at this juncture the Captain saw the glistening of a knife as the little squaw cut the rope that bound Gray Eagle. With one bound she lit astride the horse; she looked back with a frightened but determined look, the light of the fire fully reflected on her features and at the same time she gave Gray Eagle a sharp, keen cut with her quirt, and was gone with the speed of the wind, but not before a keen eye had marked the direction which she took, and the Captain said, "Now Selum here is your chance to try your full mettle. The noble horse seemed to know what was expected of him, and setting his eyes and ears on the flying object he bounded forward as if to do or die in the struggle of speed, blood and endurance. His rider held him firm and hard so that he would not over jump himself at the start, for he had every confidence in blood of man or horse. The race was up one of the beautiful valleys of Valley Creek

BIG FOOT, THE NOTED KIOWA CHIEF

without rock or bush and nothing to fear except the numerous prairie dog holes that these valleys are noted for.

For the first half mile Selum held his own with the almost flying Gray Eagle, and each jump after that distance lessened the space between the two horses, and at the distance of about one mile Selum had closed up along by the side of Gray Eagle and his rider. At that moment the little woman raised her arm to strike with the knife that she still held in her hand, but before she could strike the Captain struck her arm with a sudden blow from the heel of his clenched fist and the knife fell to the ground. He then leaned forward and straightened out his arm to grasp the bridle, but at that moment Selum's right forefoot plunged into a prairie dog hole and he fell with such force that he slid forward on the ground, and the Captain was thrown ten or fifteen feet in his advance and struck the ground with such force that he was knocked senseless. How long he remained in that condition he does not know, but when consciousness partly returned to him he raised himself to a sitting position, wondering where he was and how he got there.

Finally he rose to his feet and rubbed himself to see if he was altogether without broken bones, and then everything came back to him, the fight, the race, and his bending forward to catch the bridle of the "pretty little squaw," and then everything was a blank. After he recovered he looked around and saw his horse Selum resting his weight on three feet, his right fore foot merely touching the ground. The Captain walked up to him and gently patting him on the neck said, "Selum, are you hurt?" He uttered his low peculiar whinny, which he was accustomed to do when his rider petted and patted him. Captain Jeff then said, "Selum, my boy, you made a noble run for Gray Eagle and his rider but the fates, in this instance, as in many others, were against us, and I suppose we will have to submit to their decision, and let Gray Eagle carry the little squaw to Fort Sill to report to the Quaker agents that the big Kiowa chief did not get away with captives, scalps or horses this time. Come on, my boy, and we will go back and get the report of the boys, and I will eat some of that good beef old Big Foot was having cooked for us, for he did not know that there would be a 'slip between the cup and the lip,' but such there is with all of us." So saying, he walked back, Selum following, limping along as best he could.

When he got back to the Indian fire where the charge was made, all the other boys had done their work and were anxiously awaiting his return and they greeted him with a prolonged cheer.

He said, "Bravo! Boys, I see you are all here, and I see too that Big Foot and some of his braves are here, but they are hors de combat at last, and as we can't do anything with our horses here where they smell the blood of these Indians, gather up a lot of that barbecued beef and we will go down the creek a piece to where we can quiet our horses, eat something and all make our reports," which program was carried out at once. A camp was soon selected, horses cared for, guards placed, supper eaten, and the Captain then said, "Now for the reports; Corporal Sackett, as you went with me to the south of the fire, we will hear your report first."

Corporal Henry Sackett's report:

The Indian that was on guard with Big Foot was allotted to me didn't run and try to mount his horse, but stood firm, and when I got in some thirty feet of him he shot with his bow and my horse fell, and as my horse fell I fired at him and he dropped his bow; (which was caused from Sackett's first shot cutting off three of his fingers from the hand in which he held his bow) when my horse fell I sprang to my feet and he was running to the creek bank, and just as he was disappearing in the bushes on the creek bank I took the best aim I could and fired. I thought he fell forward, but when I got to the place he was gone."

Lieut. Best's report:

According to orders we charged north of the fire. The five Indians that were cooking sprang for their horses, two of them fell before they got to their horses, the other three succeeded in mounting and as their horses were fresh ones and good ones at that, they just simply outran us. We tried to bring them down as they ran, but we do not know whether we hit any of them or not. As the Captain's report has already been written in this connection, we think it just to give more than a passing notice to Corporal Henry Sackett. He was a young English gentleman, not only by birth and education, but a gentleman in every sense of the word, and had been schooled in horsemanship in the "old country," in riding fox and steeple chases. and was endowed by nature with all the requisites to make him a dashing and chivalrous Texas Ranger. To the other boys who were to the manor born such occurrences as herein recorded were as a matter of course as they always run the Indians one way or another.

Next morning on examination of the battle ground Big Foot and his horse lay side by side, two other Indians lay between the fire and where their horses were tied. On examination of the spot where Sackett's Indian went down the bank of the creek blood was found, and on further search a moan was heard and the party uttering the moan was found which proved to be Sackett's Indian.

He spoke good Spanish and asked for water which was soon brought to him. He drank heartily and it seemed to relieve him.

Mexican Joe was called up and he and the Captain (the Captain spoke good Spanish and Joe good English) questioned him.

He said that he was a Comanche and that the dead chief was a Kiowa; he said his own name was Jape or Japey, but he could not be persuaded in any way to tell the chief's name. He said they had left Fort Sill a few days before and that for many years they had been coming down into the settlements killing, capturing and robbing the settlers; that they were the party that killed the Johnson family, the Blaylock family, Bill Williams' family and killed Tom Milligan in Mason county so near his house, and captured and carried Miss Tod into captivity, and had carried one of Bill Williams' little girls some two hundred miles and hung her by the neck to a tree limb and left her hanging. This proved to be true for a party followed the Indians and found the little girl just as the Indian said. At this juncture of his confession Bill Williams drew his gun to shoot him in the head but he was prevented from doing so as every indication showed that he could live but a few minutes longer, for Sackett's shot was fatal. As soon as the breath left his body Bill Williams scalped him, and nobody could blame him for it. Reader, would you deprive such little revenge of that heartbroken husband and father?

Mexican Joe scalped the others and seemed very proud of his trophies. The other Indians did not get away with any horses save the ones they rode, so the Captain and Sackett had several to pick from and they got very good mounts, and moved slowly back to camp, Selum limping along following.

Cheer after cheer rent the air when our little party of nine rode into headquarters camp all well and sound in body and limb, bringing with them the trophies of their victory at last over the band that had eluded their grasp so many times.

The wiley chief's arms and marks of rank were hung up by his scalp as attests that his raids were indeed ended. His arms consisted of a Spencer breechloading rifle, a Remington army six-shooter, bow and arrow, beautifully decorated, butcher knife and shield.

Ornaments of rank—First, breast ornament made out of the second joints of human fingers of those he had killed in battle and otherwise to the number of **eighty-two joints**; second, fine headdress of eagle feathers and white women's hair.

# CHAPTER XIV.

**The Buffalo Hunt. Discipline and a Lesson Taught that Military Organization Could Profit by its Example.**

And now, kind reader, the long and cherished object of this company was at last accomplished, to-wit: the breaking up and partial destruction and total annihilation of a band of the most successful, daring and desperate Indians commanded by Big Foot, the Kiowa chief, and Jape, the Comanche, who were protected and shielded by the U. S. Government and its Quaker agents, knowingly or unknowingly, long after they were placed on the Fort Sill reservation, and the government is in duty bound to justly indemnify settlers for their losses of property and deaths that they sustained by the hands of the wards of the government, the Kiowas and Comanches, located at Fort Sill in the Indian Reservation bordering on the line of Texas

It is now October in the details of our narative, and the weather is getting cold, and our commander ever on the alert for the good of his men as well as the public service, ordered a scout of twenty men, with wagon and team, for the double purpose of making a scout and at the same time killing buffaloes for their hides to spread in the tents to sleep on.

The third evening after leaving camp on Elm creek some ten miles above where the town of Balinger now stands, buffaloes were discovered in abundance, and the scout camped at once for the night as the spot was a beautiful place for camp purposes.

The next morning the Captain left two men to guard the camp and took twenty men with him and rode to an elevation that overlooked the valleys and there to their delight was quietly grazing in the valley near them a large heard of mostly old bulls, the very kind that furnish the best hides for what they wanted.

Here the Captain placed nine men under Sergeant Mather and ten under Sergeant Moreland and told them to charge the big fellows and see which party could kill the most, saying, "I will keep Bill Williams here with me on guard. We can see all over the country with our field glasses." And now, reader, lend me your imaginations to help picture this never-to-be-forgotten buffalo charge. Imagine nineteen young, dashing, Texas Rangers, mounted on superb, fleet-footed horses, well trained to battle and firearms each man armed with a breechloading Sharp's carbine and a Colt's army six-shooter, and each man ambitious of distinction and desirous of applause. See them dashing down a beautiful little slope for some two hundred yards with the speed of a hurricane to a nice smooth valley that was covered with a monarch herd of buffaloes that were so taken by surprise by the suddenness of the charge that they could not run in any particular direction, consequently the Rangers had buffaloes before them, buffaloes behind them, buffaloes between them, and hail never fell faster than leaden pellets of death and pain entered the bodies of those victims of man's greed and cruelty. And now the fight is on in earnest. The old bulls, maddened with pain, lower their heads, raise their tails high in the air and lunge with speed and desperation at their assailants, but the fleet-footed horse, quick eye and horsemanship of his rider eludes the mad plunge in every instance; finally some of the buffaloes lead off and the rest follow them. Each man then selects a fine specimen and each pursues his victim until the nineteen selected specimens are brought down. Bill Dunman, not to be outdone, roped a fine one and tied it to a tree for breakfast next morning.

After the heard had moved off the ground where they were first attacked, two monarchs of the herd that had escaped unhurt remained on the ground with heads and tails high, rearing, pitching, sniffing, pawing and bellowing, as much as to say, "come and tackle us," which banter was more than human nature could stand and our Captain did what he never allowed one of his men to do and go unpunished (broke his orders). In this instance he said, "Bill (to the man he had kept with him on guard), we'll go and kill them two big fellows that seem to be daring us; I will take that big fellow on the left, his hide is mine; you take the other for your hide." So saying, the dash was made, and in five seconds Selum took his rider close to the side of the monster of his kind, and a ball was driven into his body behind the shoulder, and another and another; when the huge bull lowered his head and threw his tail high in the air and made a lunge at Selum (such as no other animal that ever lived could make), the horse was the twinkling of an eye the quickest; he raised Selum's tail on his horns and the horse and rider passed beyond his reach.

This fight as it were was kept up with many repetitions of the first attack until the Captain had loaded and emptied his six-shooter three times and aiming for each shot to take effect just behind the animal's left four shoulder. The shots were all fired at no greater distance than from ten to thirty feet, and he was considered the best shot with a six-shooter either running or standing in the company or out of it. So when he had shot the monster eighteen times and he still fought as determinedly as he did at first, the Captain became superstitious and thought the spirit of Big Foot or some other demon had entered into whatever it was, and that it could not be killed, so he slowly rode off and didn't get the hide to adorn his tent.

By the time he got back to where the slaughter commenced the boys had all killed each one his picked buffalo and had assembled for further orders. One man was dispatched back to camp for wagon and team, butcher knives, whetstones, etc., and the skinning was commenced and kept up until the wagon was loaded down with the best of buffalo hides, and moved back to camp late in the evening. The camp was put in military order, which was always the first thing with this company, whether there was danger of Indians or not. A bountiful supper was prepared and eaten, as their appetites had been keenly whetted by the exciting scenes and labors of the day.

After supper the Captain said: "Boys, it has been my painful duty on some occasions to punish some of you for disobedience of orders, and I broke my own orders to-day, as you all remember. I placed myself and Bill Williams on guard while you were to kill buffaloes, and then I left my post of duty, which is a very serious charge in military discipline, and as there is no higher officer here to assess my punishment, I herewith appoint all of you as a military court o pass sentence on me for violating orders." They all spoke as one man: "Why, Captain, we all would have done what you did had we been placed in your position." But said he, "That does not alter the case, an order has been broken, and the offender must be punished. Military law and the spirit of Christianity are strictly at variance, and all well-balanced and thinking minds should devoutly pray for the time to come spoken of by the meek and lowly Nazarene that the sword should be beaten into the ploughshare and the spear into the pruning hook, and that man should learn war no more, but until that times does come military law, like the laws of the Medes and Persians, must be ineorable. As you all are in a position to practice the spirit of forgiveness, I am not so situated, and as commander of this company, if I break my own orders, I must undergo the same punishment that I would have been compelled to have meted out to any one of you; therefore I put myself on solitary spy duty for two days, while you all stretch the hides and prepare them to be taken back to camp."

So the next morning the Captain saddled his horse, took a canteen of water and a lunch for his dinner and rode some two miles to an elevation that gave a good view of the surrounding country, and with his field glasses he vigilantly scanned the surroundings until the sun was set when he mounted and rode back to camp where he was greeted by many exclamations of respect by his men, for in this instance the lesson was fully demonstrated why the Captain had always exacted a strict obedience to all orders, as that is the first requisite to success in all military organizations, and that he had never demanded double duty of any of them that he was not bound to perform if he violated his own orders. Then they all said: "We will all try never to break an order under any circumstances; but should our human nature be too weak to stand the ordeal under which we may be placed, we will never think it a hardship or degrading to perform extra duty commensurate with the offense, as you have so manfully and honorably explained."

The next morning the Captain carried out to the letter his duty of the day before and his servitude for violating his own orders was completed. On his return into camp that evening he said:

# CHAPTER XV.

### The Reduction and Discharge of the Companies and Fifty Men from Each Company in the Frontier Battalion and the Return Home to it Peaceful Pursuits.

"Boys, for my part, I don't care how soon the order comes for us to be mustered out of this service. We have accomplished the main point or the particular object that caused me to accept a commission to raise and command this company, as you all know it was to utterly break up Big Foot and his bloody band of Kiowas and Comanches that have been depredating upon our homes, lives and property for so many years, and since the Civil War have been protected by the United States Government and its Quaker agents, which is proven by the dying confession of old Jape, and the many nice blankets branded U. S. that we captured with them. I told my wife when I left home that my destiny in this last drama of soldier life for the last nine years was to be filled, and as the preachers say I was called to perform a certain work, and that when that was accomplished, I would return to her and the children sound in body and mind, mounted on my horse Selum, and would find them all well; and my guardian spirit seems to say that very soon we will have an opportunity to return to our homes and their loved inmates."

The next morning the hides were packed in the wagon and in two days headquarters camp was reached, and as the Captain had predicted, there was an order from the Adjutant General's office to Captain Jeff to leave twenty-five men in charge of Second Lieutenant Foster and to report to Adjutant General's office with the balance of the company for final settlement.

The next day the men were given an opportunity to volunteer to stay and only twenty-five would stay. The next thing was an equal distribution of the trophies taken in battle. The Captain put them up in separate articles to the highest bidder, only members of the company being allowed to bid, he excluding himself from the contest, although he very much wanted Big Foot's paraphernalia, and he said long afterwards that he would have willingly bid one hundred dollars for them, but he did not want his men to know that he would take advantage of them by being able to outbid them. The sales were all made and they amounted to one hundred and eleven dollars, which was equally divided pro rata among all the men and his command of Company E, Texas Rangers was duly turned over to Lieutenant Foster, and he and his fifty men, who had prepared to go out of service with him, bade a kindly adieu to their comrades and in a few days presented themselves to Adjutant General Steel for discharge and final settlement; and they were highly complimented by said officer for doing valuable and efficient service. In this connection it is due the men to show the esteem in which they held their Captain. They bought the finest suit of clothes that could be found in the city of Austin, costing seventy-five dollars, took them to the hotel and compelled him to put them on and parade the streets with them. Two days after this Selum proudly carried his rider up to his front gate, the home in tact, and the noble wife and sweet children well and happy, with all the whisperings of the "still small voice" fully and completely verified. And so ends the military career of the man of whom we write, and so to speak, he fulfilled his promise to his devoted wife—he beat his pistol into the plough share and his sword into the pruning hook and tries to learn war no more. Shortly after this he moved from Burnet County, where he was so unjustly persecuted.

## CHAPTER XVI.

### Retrospective View.

Reader, go back with me while we chronicle very briefly a few incidents in the life of this man before this recital began.

In 1846 and 1847 he was a volunteer in Captain Felch's Company, Gray's Battalion, Arkansas Volunteers. In 1849 to 1855, inclusive, he was in the Quartermaster's employ, U. S. A. as teamster, carpenter, wagonmaster, scout, dispatch-bearer, etc., and, like David Copperfield, "doer of all odd jobs." He was at the location and helped to build most of the old Government posts on the frontier of Texas. In 1855 he was sent on a scout with Major Ruff, of the U. S. Rifles, to guard the road running from San Antonio to El Paso and near Eagle Springs the command had a fight with the Muscalry

Indians, in which ten of the Indians were killed. He captured a little girl child, its mother having been killed in the fight.

He took fatherly care of the little captive for some months. When the command reached San Elizario, a little Mexican town on the Rio Grande, he bought material to make it some clothes and gave it to a Mexican woman, as he could not take care of it on the long scout that was before them. Some time after this he wrote to inquire about his little captive. He was informed that it had sickened and died and its little spirit had taken its flight to a better world, where no doubt its murdered mother stood on the shore with open arms to receive the spirit of her little girl.

We now return and follow him to the place which he has selected for his new home. It is a beautiful basin near the geographical center of Callahan County, Texas. It is almost completely surrounded by the most beautiful and picturesque little mountains, and he christened it Mountain Dell, and to this lovely spot of God's green earth he has devoted his time and talents to the making of a lovely home. Here he has planted, pruned and cultivated with his own hands everything that is pleasing to the eye, fragrant to the smell or delicious to the palate. His house is well arranged, large and commodious, and is presided over with ease and grace and dignity by the same noble woman that has been his mainstay, comforter and counsellor through all the varying scenes which he has been called to pass through.

# CHAPTER XVII.

**Finale. At Mountain Dale, Home of Captain Jeff.**

And now in the evening of their well spent lives, reader, should you chance to visit them you will find them walking hand in hand through their orchard or vineyard or sitting on one of the many rustic seats under their own vine and fig tree, quietly worshiping the beneficent Creator for His bounties to them in giving them the opportunities and the desire to beautify the earth in the making of what might be called a Home, as a stepping stone to that

"Land that is fairer than day,
And by faith they can see it afar,
For the Father waits over the way,
To prepare them a dwelling place there."

And should you chance to make this visit to Mountain Dell, methinks I hear you exclaim: "Verily, verily, Peace hath her victories as well as War, for here dwells the pioneer and enthusiastic horticulturist of Callahan County, and the surrounding counties." And to give his sentiments we must quote him in his peroration before the Farmers' Institute in an address on grape culture.

In closing his remarks he said: "Stock raising is the occupation of the barbarous and semi-barbarious nations of the earth. Manufactories are the breeders of anarchism, alcoholism, poverty and crime, but agriculture and horticulture are the handmaidens of Law and Religion everywhere. You may admire the stockman and his broad acres, with his cattle grazing on a thousand hills; you may admire the factory with its thousands of busy spindles, but what civilizing influences do they possess? But who can stand beside the tree laden with its golden fruit or the vine with its purple cluster, or the rose in its superlative loveliness, without worshiping the God that gave such gifts to man?"

In politics he is strictly Populistic, or Progressive, his religion is broad and reaches out to the ends of the earth, and embraces every kindred and tongue.

And he here wishes to put in a protest against the Grand Jury of the present day. It may have been a wise institution for many, many years, but it has outlived its usefulness and should be relegated to the rear as one of the back numbers, for it is strictly at variance with the teachings of Christ while here on earth.

He said: "It is better that ninety-nine guilty ones should go unpunished than for one innocent person to suffer."

The Grand Jurors in most cases are well meaning men and the majority of them are members of some Christian church, and in their zeal they reverse the teachings of Christ, and by their verdicts they virtually say: "It is better to make ninety-nine innocent persons prove their innocence than one guilty man should go unpunished," and this is brought about in a great measure by the attorneys who are pecuniarily interested in the number of bills, and the real justness of the bills is of minor importance, for some of them get a small fee anyway. Again, it is praiseworthy in a Grand Jury that finds the bills on the best of evidence, or the petit jury that convicts without the shadow of a doubt.

It would be truly Christian in them to sign a petition for the unfortunate victim as King Mercy from the higher tribunals, keeping ever in view those beautiful words:

"Teach me to feel another's woe,
To hide the faults I see;
That mercy I to others show,
That mercy show to me,"

for when they have passed the sentence for conviction they have fully complied with the letter of the law, and the apostle Paul says: "The letter of the law killeth, but the Spirit of the law giveth everlasting life. The Spirit of the law and the Spirit of Christianity is forgiveness, that we in turn be forgiven by the author of it, needs be that offenses must come," whereby a standard of right could be established.

Again he thinks that capital punishment is wrong, and should be abolished, for if the laws of the United States had never adopted the cruel penalty of hanging, then mob law in this direction would have been unknown and never resorted to. In this instance the passage of Scripture is fully illustrated that sayeth, "The parents eat sour grapes and the children's teeth are on edge."

Every man that the creative power allows to be born into this world and commits a crime should be allowed one chance to reprieve his fallen character, "for of such is the kingdom of Heaven." And now our little narrative is drawing to a close; it has not been written to point a moral or adorn a tale, but to chronicle in a plain, brief way some unwritten facts which have contributed their "widow's mite" in making West Texas what it is today, and if perchance it should be read by some young men and women and they should try to emulate the peaceful pursuits of these worthy old people, then the world will be bettered by their having lived in it. And know, dear reader, they bid you a kind adieu, while they wait for the call from the Land of the Leal where they expect to sit down and smoke the pipe of peace with Big Foot and all the nations of the earth, fully recognizing and acknowledging the universal Fatherhood of God and brotherhood of man.

JAPE, THE COMMANCHIE

# Capt. Maltby Honored

Captain W. J. Maltby, Admiral, Texas: My Dear Captain—At a meeting in the city of Dallas, some time back, by the Ex-Rangers of this State, I had the pleasure of nominating you as historian, which was agreed to. I have no doubt that you have been duly notified of your selection for this important position, and truly hope you will acept it.

While it was only my pleasure to have been one of your command for a few months, as a member of Company E, Frontier Battalion, my association with you fully satisfied me that you had, from actual experience, a vast storehouse of information relating to frontier life, which, if portrayed on paper, would be very interesting to those who wish to read it.

The many risks and hazards the early frontiersman had to contend with, taking his life constantly in his hands, living on the confines of civilization, helping and assisting in rendering more secure the lives and property of those who were pushing along at your very heels, feeling assured by the knowledge that in front of them lived men inured to frontier life, safeguarding their lives and property, without fear or care, from the encroachment of raiding and desperate bands of Indians—this you can surely portray. While the history of the frontier of Texas, from the Rio Grande on the South to the Red River on the North, inseparably binds together the lives of the hardy frontiersman and the Texas Ranger as one, their many deeds of valor and daring, if written, will speak of the many grand old heroes that fought and fell; also of those who, in some marvelous way, escaped alive, though battle-scarred. And amongst these your name, as one who had risked his all in the many and various trials incident thereto, will stand with the foremost as having donated your full quota of service in assisting to develop the Western part of Texas, making life and property safe and secure as it now is, to-day, unequaled in any other part of the State. The history of the services rendered by the Texas Ranger to this great State of ours is, or would be, if fully portrayed, of the greatest interest to many citizens of our great. State. Many to-day, living safe and secure in their quiet country homes, would kindly remember and do honor to those who, by devotion to duty, by constant, continuous service, as Rangers, ready to cope with any emergency, at any time or place, had made possible these conditions, repeating the history of the growth and development of all of this great country of ours from the beginning.

It would seem that in the years 1874 and 1875, during Governor Coke's administration, the most efficient and effective Ranger service was furnished by the State, and her Frontier Battalion, under Major John B. Jones' command, finally and for all time served notice on the raiding bands of Indians that their day of raiding, stealing and killing on the frontier of Texas was forever and eternally a thing of the past. The rapid settlement and organization of about twenty-five counties (I think) on the line of the battalion's base of action, co-incident with this date, is surely proof enough that the State was effectually cleared of any Indian danger and that the newly-opened country was safe and secure to all comers. Company E, which you commanded, and of which I was one, surely did its full duty, equal at least to the duties performed by the other five companies.

To you and men of your type distinctly belong the honor and credit, fontiersman and ranger, of effectualy driving from our frontier the hostile Indian who tried men's souls. I take off my hat in honor to such men, tried and true, and never found wanting.

Captain, I hope to live to enjoy reading your reminiscences, if you decide to write them. With the highest personal regards, I beg to remain your friend, HENRY SACKETT.

Admiral. Texas, Dec. 17, 1904.

# Capt. Maltby's Reminiscences.

## CHAPTER I.

The first man with whom I shall deal in this article is Major Jones, commander of the Frontier Battalion.

He was a man endowed with excellent judgment, his bravery was unquestioned, and he soon proved himself in every way qualified to fill the responsible position to which Governor Coke had appointed him. On his first visit to the camp of Company E, which camp was on Clear Creek, some twelve miles west of the present town of Brownwood, he called on me for six men to form part of his escort. He also called on the other companies for a like number of men to form a scout from one company to the other, and this scout passed continuously back and forth along the line, and made one of the most effective patrols ever instituted on the frontier.

On the Major's first trip along the line a band of one hundred Indians, all of them well armed, charged into his command, and here his coolness, bravery and excellent judgment saved his company from a complete annihilation. He succeeded in getting his men into a ravine and whipped the Indians off. In this fight each of the six men from Company E had his horse shot from under him, and one of the men was severely wounded in the leg. The fight was known as the Las Valley fight.

Jack Hays commanded the first company of Rangers that was armed with Colt's five shooters and cap and ball pistols. The territory that he ranged over was from San Antonio north and west over the waters of the Medina, Rio Frio, Hondo, Savinal, Nueces, etc., and he did as valuable services in the years of 1844 and 1845 as ever has been done for the frontier of Texas. In 1846 he was ordered with his Company to join Gen. Taylor with his company who was then rendezvousing on the Rio Grande preparatory to making his advance into Mexico. When Capt. Hays presented himself and company to Gen. Taylor for duty, the general was well posted in the intrepidity of Captain Hays and his company, which was then known and recognized as Texas Rangers. Gen. Taylor had immediate use for Capt. Hays and his intrepid Rangers, so he placed them on duty as his particular Spy Company to penetrate the enemy's country, to locate their army, to watch and dog their movements, and report to him from time to time with such information as might be valuable to him in his advance, and this service could not have been allotted to more valiant, worthy and intrepid men than Jack Hays and his Texas Rangers. Before the battle of Palo Alto the General sent Hays out to reconnoitre the Mexican's position, and in this instance Captain Hays' headlong intrepidity caused him to penetrate so far into the Mexican lines that before he was aware of the fact, a large force of Mexican cavalry had him almost surrounded and cut off from Gen. Taylor's army. This was the most trying place that our Captain had ever been in, and probably the first time in his life he ever tried to pray, but as something had to be done, and that quickly, he offered up this prayer : " Almighty God, be on our side if you can, but if you can't, for Christ's sake don't be on theirs. But stand off on one of these hills and look, and you'll see the damdest fight you ever saw in your life." And in place of saying "Amen!" he said "Charge, boys! Charge!" and they burst their way through the Mexican lines like a hurricane through a canebrake, with the loss of only three men killed and four wounded, none mortally.

Captain Jack Hays' descriptive list would read thus (at the time that the writer formed his acquaintance, which was at San Antonio in 1852 or 1853) : 35 years of age, 6 feet high, spare build, weight 150 or 160, rather dark complexion, and by occupation a bona fide Texas Ranger.

Capt. William (alias Big Foot) Wallace, was one of the grand and noble old Romans that contributed more than the "widow's mite" to wresting from the bloody and barbarous Comanche and Kiowa Indians this fair land of West Texas, that is destined in the near future to be the happy and prosperous home of thousands and tens of thousands of happy and contented people. Captain Wallace was one of the unfortunate Mier prisoners who were subject to the brutality of Santa Anna, "the Napoleon of the West," as he termed himself, to which reference is made in Mrs. Anna J. H. Pennybacker's History of Texas, page 112 to 116, which shows that Capt Wallace was one of the fortunates that drew a white bean for his life. Capt. Wallace participated in all the memorable battles of '46 and '47 under Gen. Taylor and meted out to the enemy a just reward for their barbarous cruelties to himself and his comrades while they were Mier prisoners.

After the war of 1846-7, Capt. Wallace made his home on the Madena west of San Antonio, and gave most of his time and talent to the protection of that section which was continually raided by Indians and Mexican outlaws. When the overland stage was started from San Antonio to El Paso Capt. Wallace was employed to take command of the expedition. This was very hazardous and none but the toughest, most daring and resoluate men were employed to go as guards and mule whackers, as some five hundred miles of this road was exposed to the continued depredations of the Indians.

On one of these trips a man by the name of Jim Clark was employed for his man eating qualities. Captain gave him some order to which he took offense whereupon he whipped out his six shooter in a bullying and braggadocio manner. The only notice Capt. Wallace made to Clark's beligerent action was to speak in his slow, drol manner and say, "Jim, you'd better put up that gun, damn fools and boys have no business to fool with pistols, for they are liable to let them go off accidentally and hurt somebody." The writer kept the stage stand at Fort Clark and on the return trip Clark told me the incident just as written. Clark said: "That cooked me more than anything that ever happened to me, and it has learned me a lesson, that I will never draw my pistol on a brave man again, and I would follow old Big Foot wherever he leads, yes, to the jumping off place, and if it needs be, jump off with him."

Capt. Wallace had perfect command over himself and all those that were placed under him. The stage was attacked several times while in charge of Capt. Wallace, but his bravery and good generalship always whipped the Indians off, and he brought in the mail on regular time.

In the year 1856 Capt. Wallace went in charge of a large train of eight mule teams loaded with merchandise from San Antonio to Chihuahua. On his return trip the writer fell in with him at Old Fort Lancaster on the Pecos river and traveled with him some two hundred miles, and one night while sitting in camp I said to Capt. Wallace, "how did you get the name of "Big Foot?" Your foot is in fair proportions to your size, as a man." He replied, "well, as we have been acquainted for some years, and you know that I am not given to boasting of deeds performed when and where I could not help myself, I will tell you."

"For years I was one of a party that followed the Indians when they raided our country and from time to time the trails showed that one of them made a much larger track than the others and it was generally supposed that he was the Big Foot Indian and "mucha bravo." Well, to make a long story short, the Indians came in and killed two or three persons, and stole a bunch of horses and struck out as usual. We gathered up some fifteen men and struck out after them. We pressed hard after them for five days when we camped just at, or near dark, and about the same time some of our party discovered a fire around the bend of the creek; it was then decided that we all keep perfectly quiet and not make any fire, and I proposed to go very stealthily forward, and spy out the camp and its surroundings, which I started to do.

At once my course was up a narrow, shallow ravine that was rather smooth in the bottom, with thick brush on each side. About half way from where I started to the Indian fire, the little ravine made a short, abrupt turn, and then went on up to where the Indians were camping. I suppose that about the time that I started to spy out the Indian camp, the big Indian started back to find out if they were followed. At all events, we met just at the short turn in the ravine. I can't tell how it was, or why, unless it was so ordered but it seemed as if by mutual consent we both dropped our guns and rushed together. I threw my entire weight and strength against him, which forced him back. His foot caught on some obstruction and we fell, my whole weight on his breast, which seemed for the moment to have knocked the breath out of him. In an instant I drew my knife and drove it into his breast, once, twice, thrice, with all the speed and strength that I could command, and he died without a groan. I rose to my feet trembling and perfectly exhausted, and I fervently tried to thank Kind Providence for allowing me to draw another *white bean*. I picked up my gun and went slowly back to camp and by the time I got back to camp my strength and nerve had greatly revived, so much so that I was able to explain what had happened, and what I supposed would be the proper mode of making the advance on the Indians.

My plan was approved and I said, "All follow me, and don't speak above a whisper or break a dry twig, if you can help it." We all moved cautiously up the little ravine that seemed to have been made for this special occasion, passed the curve and over the dead Indian, and straight forward to the Indian fire.

We approached to within some one hundred yards of the fire without making any alarm, and here we had a pretty good view of the fire around which eight buck Indians sat roasting beef. I whispered to my men to take the very best aim they could and at the crack of my gun to all fire, which was nicely done, and four big bucks fell over, some of them into the fire, the other four sprang to their feet, dashed into the thick brush, and were gone. We reloaded our guns, and walked up to the fire, picked up the sticks of meat they were cooking, left the dead Indians just as they fell, and went back to our horses, unsaddled them, each man staked out his own horse, sat down by him, ate his piece of Indian beef and remained in that position until morning.

When good daylight came we saddled up, went around the way the Indians went the evening before and rode up to the fire, where everything was just as we left it, only the Indians that fell in the fire were pretty well cooked. As our appetites had no cravings for such meat, and as there was plenty of good beef hanging on a tree that was left the evening before, we each one cut a piece to suit himself, tied it to his saddle and then moved down the fatal little ravine (to the Indian).

When we got down to the curve where I drew my second white bean, on examination we found that my special antagonist of last night was the Big Foot Indian, and so the men with one accord hurrahed for Captain "Big Foot Wallace," and the name has stuck to me ever since and I gratefully and thankfully accept it as another "white bean" in the prolongation of my earthly existence."

Descriptive list of Capt. William (alias Big Foot) Wallace: Six feet two inches high, weight two hundred to two hundred and twenty-five pounds, beard and hair black and very heavy. Eyes blue, and by occupation, like Daniel Boone and Davy Crockett, a frontiersman, and one of God's noblemen. His disposition was that of a child, in peace, but terrible and destructive as a lion in war.

## CHAPTER II.

Col. John S. (Rip) Ford. To follow this man through the battles of the Mexican war of 1846 and 1847, and his councils in peace in the legislative halls, and his prowess as a soldier on the battlefield as a Texas Ranger in Central and West Texas, and the border troubles on the Rio Grande, would require a volume, and must be left to a more gifted pen than mine, although the writer has been with Col. Ford in some of his military expeditions when valuable service was performed for both the State and the Confederate States.

It will suffice to say that he was a minature Washington; first in war, first in peace, and first in the hearts of his frontiersmen. He seemed to carry a charmed life that was proof against shot, shell, fire or the sword; for he passed through a long and eventful career with but little bodily harm, and died at a green and mellow old age, at his home, surrounded by a loving family and friends, and had the very highest respect of all who knew him personally, and left a bright and brilliant star in the galaxy of the Texas Ranger.

Col. Ford's descriptive list: Six feet high, weight one hundred and seventy-five pounds. Compelxion light, blue eyes. Occupation, editor, doctor, representative, soldier, statesman, typical Texas Ranger.

## CHAPTER III.

Gen. Henry McCullough, soldier ranger and patriot. This man was another bright cloud that hung over the frontier of Texas for so many long and weary years. This man's service as a ranger, citizen and patriot was equal to any and inferior to none, and the name McCullough will be inscribed on the pages of Texas history as one of its grand and noble defenders.

Here is a little incident in his life as related by himself in regard to the strength of the bridle having something to do with the speed of the horse, particularly when in pursuit of a deadly foe.

Once upon a time when Captain McCullough commanded a company of Rangers, he was in hot pursuit of a band of Indians when a Mexican fell in with him riding apparently a very worthless pony. The Captain said to him, "Your pony is worthless and can't keep up." The Mexican replied: "Kin sava, senior, yo pienco K see."

The Indians were soon sighted, and the Ranger charge was made, and as ridiculous as it may appear the Mexican's worthless little pony outran the Captain's horse from start to finish. After the fight was over the Captain inquired of the Mexican how it was possible for him to make such a pony out run his Kentucky horse. The Mexican rode up to him and with a quizzical expression beaming from his every feature, and gently taking hold of his bridle said, "Me no have strong bridle like El Capitano."

Gen. McCullough was a man of strong individuality and dared to do what he thought was right regardless of the consequences. An instance of this came within the writer's own knowledge.

In 1862 H. E. McCullough was made Brigadier General in the Confederate Army; Allen's, Waterhouse's, Randall's and Flourney's regiments formed his brigade. They were formed into the brigade near Little Rock, Ark., where Gen. McCullough issued an order that no man should kill a hog, and that if any man was caught killing a hog he would have him dishonorably drummed out of the camp.

A few days after, two men were caught killing a hog. The General at once had the brigade formed in two lines facing each other, a space of say fifteen feet between them, placed the prisoners at the head of the column with four men of the guard in the attitude of charge bayonets behind them, and with drum and fife, had them marched down the lines with music fitted to the words:

"Poor old soldier, poor old soldier,
 Tarred and feathered and sent to hell
 Because he broke an order," etc.

The General had the brigade formed into a hollow square facing inwards. He rode into this square and taking off his hat, said: "Officers and men of this brigade, I am sorry that my sense of duty and discipline compelled me to carry out this seemingly tyrannical order, but as commander of this brigade, my orders must be obeyed as long as I command it. I hope the brigade will stand by me in doing what I conceived to be the best for the good of the service and the protection of the citizens and their property. If you do not approve of my actions, then I will stand alone in doing what I think is right. All that will stand by me will step one step forward." He then gave the command "march" and the entire brigade stepped one step forward, and he was unanimously exonerated. He still rode his fine Kentucky horse with a *strong bridle*.

Descriptive list of Gen. Henry E. McCullough: Five feet 10 inches high, light complexion, blue eyes; weight one hundred and fifty pounds. Occupation, farmer, stock raiser, ranger, soldier, patriot.

## CHAPTER IV.

Gen. John R. Baylor. This name stands in the front rank of frontier heroes as ranger, frontiersman, soldier, patriot and statesman.

This man's operations were in Central and North Texas and he did as much in driving back and holding the Indians in check as any other. He was well versed in the use of all the fire arms of his day, and in additon he was a perfect expert with the historical arms of the Indians, the bow and arrow, and the lance, which he always carried with him when scouting for Indians. He always killed the meat for his scouting party with the bow and arrow as the report of fire arms would oftimes give the Indians the direction of his whereabouts. Like Big Foot Wallace, he was a man of powerful physique, and could run his horse along by the side of a large buffalo, and drive an arrow through its body. In the years of 1858-9 the government placed the Comanche and Kiowa Indians on the reservation at Camp Cooper on the Clear Fork of the Brazos, and placed officers and soldiers to protect them with arms, cannon, etc. The government fed and clothed and protected them, but did not keep them from raiding the unprotected white settlers, which was borne by the white settlers until forbearance ceased to be a virtue, and so they prayed for a commander to lead them against Camp Cooper and wipe it from the face of the earth—as far as its occupants were concerned. Their prayers were answered in the person of Capt. John R. Baylor, a Texas Ranger of true and tried ability, who was ever ready to lead a forlorn hope for the good of his suffering and unfortunate people.

That winter James M. Lovett and Wilson Light and myself had gone to the Wichita Mountains to join Maj. Earl Vandorn, who had been ordered to that locality by the United States Government to make a determined onslaught against the Indians that were reported to be congregating in great numbers in the Wichita mountains.

When the writer's little party of three reached Maj. Vandorn's camp which was located at the south base of the mountains on the head of the creek called Sandy, the Major had gone on a scout in which he took an Indian camp by surprise and killed fifty warriors and piled them up in one pile. He lost several of his men, killed and wounded, among whom was Lieut. Radsminsky, who heroically lost his life to save the life of his commanding officer—Maj. Earl Vandorn.

When Maj. Vandorn returned to camp he named the camp Radsminsky in honor of his lieutenant, who so heroically gave his life to save the life of his commanding officer. Here the writer formed the acquaintance of Sol B. Davis, a nephew of Jefferson Davis, who was the Secretary of War. Sol B. Davis carried with him an order from the Secretary of War to any commanding officer of government posts to turn over to the said Sol B. Davis any number of soldiers for escort, or any government property to suit his

pleasure or convenience. Sol B. Davis had just come out to Vandorn's camp from Fort Arbuckle, where he had obtained a lieutenant and twenty soldiers for an escort, two six mule teams, wagons,
tents, and other camp accessories.

His own private traveling equipage consisted of a very fine
ambulance with a five hundred dollar pair of mules to draw it, a
man to drive it, a fine saddle horse and saddle mule and a negro
cook, and all kinds of firearms up to date, with tobacco, pipes and
whiskey galore. Myself and Light were pressingly invited to join
him in his buffalo hunts, and as he had wagons, teams, tents and
soldiers to guard us while in camp we cheerfully accepted the invitation, since we were well mounted, well armed and out for venture,
fun or frolic.

In these hunts many things happened, but we will relate one that
was not so very funny. It was on Cash creek, below where Fort
Sill is now located. We had camped on the creek. Davis, Light
and myself went up the creek some three or four miles to kill just
such buffalo as we might fancy. Davis rode his fine horse, bought
for this very purpose. Light and myself rode the best of Texas
horses. Some four miles from camp we discovered a bunch of
buffalo just to our liking, which consisted mostly of two year old
heifers that could run, *and don't you forget it.*

We wanted to give Davis a chance to try his fine horse, and to
have something that he could remember and tell when he got back
home, and we did. When we got ready to make the charge, Davis
tied his fine breech-loading rifle fast to the horn of his saddle, intending to use his six-shooter only in the run.

Light and myself were armed with Colt's army six-shooters, cap
and ball, one each. In the charge Light's horse took the lead, and the
buffalo turned and I dashed right into them and commenced firing
as fast as I could. Davis was just behind me. My firing, and the
buffalo, frightened Davis' horse which threw him, and like Brother
Crawford's horse of old, he threw his tail over his back, and said,
"Farewell, Brother Davis." The horse almost flew after he had

thrown his rider, for with his every jump the muzzle of the gun would rise and come down with a whack on his side or shoulder, and this of course drove him to his utmost speed.

We followed him with our eyes for about a mile and a half, when we saw a bunch of Indians dash in all around him. Light got off his horse, made Davis mount into the saddle, sprang up behind him and if we did not make as good time to camp as Davis' horse did after he said "Farewell, Brother Davis"—why we *almost* did, you know how it is yourself—if you have been there.

After we got to camp we summed up the casualties of the day's hunt and it stood thus: No meat, Davis' horse, bridle, saddle, gun and powder flask lost, Light and Jeff with two empty pistols and nothing to load them with. Had the Indians overtaken us we would have fallen easy pray as we had nothing for defense except Davis' six-shooter and the loads that were in it.

As Sol B. Davis would have something to remember when he got back home to Baltimore. We returned to Texas by way of Camp Cooper, and got to Camp Cooper the day after Capt. John R. Baylor made his unsuccessful attack on the Indian reservation. This wide digression was to show how the writer happened to be there the next day after the attack. If Capt. Baylor had been in command of two hundred of his old Rangers in all probability he would have been successful for the time being. But those big ugly cannon loaded to the muzzle was more than tenderfeet could attack.

The movement was productive of good results to the settlers, anyway, for it caused the government to locate Fort Sill in the Indian Reservation and move the Indians to it, which saved many lives and much property. Baylor was made a Brigadier General in the Confederate War, and before leaving San Antonio he had a nice Confederate uniform made suitable to his rank, and the ladies of San Antonio presented him with a beautiful Confederate flag, both of which he prized very much.

After the war was over he lived in San Antonio for some years, and the last time the writer met him was during Gov. Coke's administration. I met him in the legisaltive hall and after the usual friendly greeting, he said, "Come, let's go down and irrigate," meaning take a drink. We walked down to an irrigation fountain and after turning down an exhilarating quantity of the "Oh, be joyful" the General said, "The doctors advise me since my last sickness to take a little stimulent pretty often." I replied, "I had not heard of your sickness." He said, "Oh, yes. I have been at death's door. The doctors all gave me up, and told Mrs. Baylor that I could not live and for her to ask me if I had any request to make before I died. She came to me with tears streaming down her cheeks, and said, 'John, have you any requests to make?' and if so, she would have them performed. I said, "Yes, if I die I want you to put me in my Confederate uniform, wrap my Confederate flag around me, and when I get over there I will walk up to Stonewall Jackson and report to him for duty." By the time this little speech was ended, tears were streaming down my cheeks.

## CHAPTER V.

### *THE LAST SKIRMISH WITH THE INDIANS ON THE RIO GRANDE, AND WHAT LED UP TO IT.*

In 1883 the United States Government had forced all of the different tribes of Indians that depredated on the frontier of Texas onto the different reservations, but still there were some roving bands of the different tribes that found a refuge in the mountain fastnesses of the Rio Grande where game and fish were abundant and where a vast country two or three hundred miles in length on either side of the river was totally uninhabited.

The Texas and Pacific Railway had crossed the western frontier and the stockmen, eager to take possession of all the water and grass, made a mad rush westward and drove their stakes and set up their claims on every available location suitable for a big stock ranch; so at the time of which I write, all of the locations worthy of note, for size, water and grass, were located and had the cattle on them, and the last and only chance to get possession of a big stock ranch lay on the Rio Grande some two hundred miles below El Paso.

Its security from location was, on acount of it being held by the different bands of uncaptured hostile Indians and Mexican marauders, spoken of at the beginning of this chapter. It was understood that thirty leagues in one body of this land, in the desirable portion belonged to one rich Mexican, and the facts and records of same could be obtained only in the city of Chichihuhua, Mexico.

Clabe eMrchant and T. B. Hadley, being very extensive stockmen, like all others, were very desirous of getting permanent possession of just such a ranch of thirty thousand acres of well watered and well grassed land, so as to graze their cattle upon a thousand hills where no one could dare to make them afraid.

The determination of the above named gentlemen was to send a representative to negotiate and get an option for twelve months on the land so as to give them time to look it over and decide as to its value as a big and permanent ranch.

The next consideration was a man that they could send forward to Chichihuhua as their representative and they both nominated Capt. Jeff as their first choice. They at once called on him and explained what they wanted and urged him to accept the mission, saying, "We will grant you any request you may make in the premises. Captain replied: "Well, gentlemen, I think your first choice of me for this mission flatters my abilty in a deal of its probable magnitude, but give me Ed S. Seay, one of my true and tried rangers, whose courage and ability has ever been equal to the occasion or the requirements, and I will undertake to carry out your mission to a successful and profitable conclusion."

As Ed S. Seay was a son-in-law of Clabe Merchant, the preliminaries for the trip were soon made, the day set to start, and the journey to Chichihuhua made without let or hindrance. The records examined, the owner found, negotiations entered into perfectly satisfactory, records made and our little party of two, very reluctantly bade adieu to the land of perpetual roses, dark eyed, blushing, senoritas, sparkling fountains, moon-lit promenades, etc.

If they had not been married men, and honor bound to return they would have been there yet. Reader, had you been with them you would have thought so too. They reached home without any incident worthy of note on the trip. Their trip was more than satisfactory to their employers, and the day was set to board the Texas and Pacific Railway at Baird, with saddle horses, pack mules and everything necessary to make a close and careful inspection of the country on both sides of the Rio Grande, both above and below (where the famous Spring of the Future is located).

The mantel of the expedition was thrown on Capt. Jeff, and he was compelled to wear it in honor of his long service and experience after Indians in this same country in the year of 1855. The party that was to go forward and view out this "promised land," if there was any such, was Clebe Merchant, Tom Hadley and our Jeff, and no truer or better men, or better shots could be found on the frontier of Texas, the natural home of the true and the brave.

Our little party of three got everything, as they thought, that they could use on the trip, but they didn't, as will be told later on, and three days before they were to start Mr. Clabe Merchant was taken sick, and his doctor said it would be impossible for him to go, so he picked one George Laird, one of his true, trusted and tried cowboys, to go in his place. So the outfit was loaded, the tickets bought for Carizo Pass, which place we reached in due time. We unloaded and took inventory of our stock and found everything we could use but a fish hook and line, which was one of the things that they would need badly, especially when they got to the Rio Grande.

So they borrowed a small perch hook and line from a lady, and Jeff said, "Boys, I will show you some expert fishing with this hook and line before we get back."

The horses were saddled, mules packed and they struck out for Eagle Springs, some fifteen miles distance, and directly on the way they wanted to go. They reached the springs and camped for the first night.

After horses were cared for and supper was eaten, Capt. Jeff said, "Boys, throughout the balance of this trip, we will each one be called by his Christian name. I will be called simply Jeff and you will be called Tom and George, the old familiar frontier style." He then said, "Boys, to while away the time, and make sleep sweeter when we do lie down, I will relate to you some of my experiences at this place, Eagle Springs, just twenty-eight years ago in this month in the spring of 1855. The Indians on this road, which runs from San Antonio to El Paso, were very troublesome and killed a great many people all along the road, and more at this place than at any other, and to protect the travel on this road, the United States Government sent Maj. Rough with one company of United States rifle men to scout up and down the road.

A train of twenty-five six-mule teams was sent with him to haul necessary supplies for a company of men for six months. The expedition started from Fort Clark. At that time and for years before I was in the quartermaster's employ as a carpenter, and had helped to build a number of the Government posts on the frontier of Texas. The Quartermaster sent me with Maj. Rough as his carpenter to keep his train of wagons in repair, so that he could keep on the move to give better protection all along the road, as this Eagle Spring was considered one of the worst places on the road, Maj. Rough put in more time here than anywhere else. The first time our command camped here, our guide, James Cloud, was telling me and the wagon master of the scenery there was back on the Rio Grande, just where we are going tomorrow.

His description was so grand and romantic that we three went to Maj. Rough and asked his permission to allow us to go back to the river and view its sceneries, to which the Major readily consented, saying, "I will send Lieut. Randal and twenty men along with you, make a scout and add business to pleasure."

The guide led off to the front and the scout followed in military procession for a distance of some twelve miles. The guide rode some little distance in advance of the scout and just as he reached the top of a ridge or hill his quick eye discovered a band of Indians at the bottom of the hill beating up mesquite beans on a large, flat rock.

He drew his horse suddenly up and motioned back, "halt." The Indians did not see him, and the top of the hill completely hid the scout from their view. Here a council of action was quickly held. Lieut. Randal, with a part of the men, the guide in the lead, was to go around them. Some were detailed to hold the horses, the others to lie down and crawl to the top of the hill, but not to show themselves and not to make any noise until the report of the guide's rifle was heard, which was carried out to the letter. The guide worked his party around to within two hundred yards of the Indians undiscovered, at which time the chief raised his head to look, and the clear, keen crack of the rifle broke the silence of the mountain air, and the chief fell back with a rifle ball through his brain.

The signal to shoot was given, and all hands tried to make a full "hand" in the massacre. For massacre it was to the poor, unfortunate victims, as they had no show for their lives, surrounded as they were.

The smoke of battle soon cleared away, and we advanced to where they fell, ten in number, and two of them were women; and there by the side of one was a beautiful little girl, some twelve or fourteen months old. We carried this little thing back to this place, and my mess had plenty of pork and beans and the little one seemed to be nearly famished and I fed her all of the pork and beans that her little stomach could hold, thinking at the time that the gorge would kill her, and she would be better off, but it never made her the least sick. I kept her and fed her the same thing day after day for two months and she fattened like a pig.

The newspapers of San Antonio made a great to do about Major Rough's ten strike and Lieutenant Randal's scalping the chief, but did not mention us that got up the scout. Had he, Major Rough, been the Indian fighter that the papers blew him up to be or had the expedition been under the command of some of the old Texas Rangers, and I could have lived to make the report, I think I could have made the report of the biggest Indian fight and the capture of the most horses and mules of any one fight on the frontier of Texas outside of General McKenzie's fight, but Major Rough was not a McKenzie, neither was he a Texas Ranger.

It was this way: After Major Rough had made this ten strike that I have just related, we moved on towards El Paso and moved on back by this place, some two months later went on down by Fort Davis and camped at what was then known as Barilla Springs, some thirty miles east of Fort Davis, and some thirty miles west of Leon Holes. As our command was pulling out of camp just as the sun was rising the next morning, we saw two lone horsemen coming to meet us, which proved to be George McClellan, a government wagonmaster, and one of his teamsters. He reported to Major Rough substantially as follows: That he had been sent from Fort Clark with nine six-mule teams and wagons loaded with supplies to be delivered at Fort Davis; that yesterday he reached the Leon Holes about noon and turned his mules loose to water and graze, placed two men to herd them; the Indians saw them coming and secreted themselves and when the mules got off a little distance from the wagons they dashed in between the mules and wagons and drove them off, all but one, which was blind in one eye and in the scare its good eye was towards the wagons and it ran to them and was saved. The teamsters all had six-shooters and they ran afoot after the Indians firing as best they could and captured several things which they made the Indians drop, among which was a beautiful blond scalp, no doubt of some pure white girl that they had captured, outraged and brutally murdered. The guide, James Cloud, and myself rode over the ground and found that there was four bands of the Indians and that they were driving as much as 1000 head of mules and horses to the band, making 4000 head in all, besides the fifty-four mules of the government train. They had so many the teamsters while running them afoot captured thirteen head of horses and mules, one of which one of the teamsters rode while the wagonmaster rode the one-eyed mule which the Indians did not get.

The wagonmaster did not know anything of Major Rough's whereabouts so he waited till dark and he and his teamsters saddled up the two mules and struck out for Fort Davis and came to us as I have stated. Major Rough moved his command on down to Leon Holes that day and camped. The next morning he ordered a scout of thirty men to take the trail and follow it thirty miles and then return. I did not hear the orders given to Lieutenant Randal so I saddled up my horse and started with the scout. After riding along six or eight miles I rode up by the side of the guide and he said: "Jeff, if I was you I would not go." I said, "Why?" He said, "We are only going to follow the Indians to-day and back to camp to-morrow, and we have no show to overtake them, and you will have two days' ride for nothing." So I turned and rode back and it proved as he said. When the scout got back the next evening I went to the guide and asked him all about it and he said: "The Indians stopped, killed and ate three government mules in going less than thirty miles," which so exasperated Garrigus, the wagon master and myself, in connection with the pretty blond scalp, that we three went to Major Rough and plead with him to let us take government mules and the teamsters who were all willing to go, and follow them and make the fight. As the guide said he was sure the Indians were no farther than the Horse Head crossing on the Pecos, their noted place to rest, eat and sleep after their long, hard raids on the frontier settlers, as they had no knowledge of Major Rough and his sixty-five well-mounted, well-armed U. S. riflemen and his thirty-seven teamsters, being in fifty miles of them and they need not have cared, as it proved. Boys, here was the best opportunity to make a historical fight and recapture 4000 head of the suffering and bleeding frontier men's horses and mules that has ever come under my observation, but it seemed that the Indians' Kind Providence sent them a Major Rough to protect them.

We will go by the place tomorrow and see if the Indians were ever found and buried. I thought then and think yet that such a killing was cruel and savage in the extreme, our only justification was and is that they would have murdered us just the same, if they had been given the opportunity that was presented to us.

## CHAPTER VI.

And now, boys, as times have changed so much in the last twenty eight years here at Eagle Springs, I think we can spread down our blankets and sleep sweetly without fear of the bloody tomahawk and scalping knife of the wily savage."

By daybreak the next morning our little party of three was up and as gay as larks and felt ready and equal to any and all emergencies that might lie in their path. Breakfast was prepared and eaten. Horses saddled, mules packed and the start made for the Rio Grande via where the Indians were slaughtered twenty-eight years before. Jeff's retentive memory of location, being a natural woodsman, enabled him to go straight to the spot where the unfortunate Indians were killed. Their bones were all there as none survided to tell the story to the rest of the tribe.

About noon they reached the river, and while Tom and George unpacked the mules and made a fire, Jeff stepped down to the river with his little perch hook and brought back a five or six pound cat fish, which, with other things, made a splendid dinner. As they had had a very hard ride in the forenoon they took a long rest and in the afternoon they saddled up and crossed the river. As the river was dry in that place, they went several miles into Mexico, and returned back at night to their first camp. As they came into camp that evening Jeff noticed a good many deer signs and he said, "Boys, I will go over there in the morning and kill a deer for breakfast."

So, next morning when it was good light he said, "Tom, saddle up a horse and when you hear me shoot come over. I will have a nice deer for you to bring back to camp." So saying he walking across the bed of the river and in a few minutes the crack of the rifle rang out clear and sharp, and Tom said, "George, Jeff has got it. I will ride over and get it, and we will have a good venison steak for breakfast." After partaking of a hearty breakfast they packed and saddled up and went down the river some miles where it made a short bend, and ran against the bluff. There was grass in the bend, and the prettiest place to fish that was ever seen.

Jeff said, "Boys, let's noon here and I will show you what an expert I am in catching big catfish with a minnow hook." So, while the boys were attending to the horses and making a big fire, Jeff cut a long willow pole, took a piece of the deer's liver and went down to the river, where he found one of the prettiest places to land a big fish with a small hook that was ever seen, and then the fun commenced, for no sooner than the bait struck the water than a nine pound cat fish had it and he was safely landed, and a second and a third in rapid succession. After cutting a willow switch and running it through their gills he carried them to the fire, and George remarked, "I'll bet my boots and make this trip bare-footed, that Jeff can catch the largest fish with the smallest hook of any man in the world." As there was more fish than enough for one meal they thought that they would have one for dinner. So Jeff soon had one dress for dinner which George fryed to a fine finish, and another good old frontier dinner was eaten.

After they were rested they saddled and packed and Jeff remarked, "I think we have more good meat than we can eat, two nine-pound catfish and a deer, but we will take it along until we get something better." They moved on down the river and found that they had nooned at the upper end of the lower Narrows where the bluffs set in two or three hundred feet high and the river bends from bluff to bluff, and there is no possible way to get through, only to cross the river at each bend, and here the river is one continuous body of water, so when our party came to the first place where they had to cross or turn back, they all dismounted to consult what to do, and going down to the water's edge lo and behold a band of Indians had crossed ahead of them, their mocassin tracks were plain in the sand where they went into the river. Here Tom and George hesitated about crossing, for forward the river looked much deeper than backwards, and we did not know but what the water was very deep. Jeff said, "Boys, I never have turned back and am not going to this time,if you will stay with me." They replied, "We come to stay, and you bet we will." Jeff then instructed them to stay and guard the horses while he waded the river, first remarking that the Indians had crossed and he could cross also. After crossing he found that it would not quite swim the pack mules. When he got to the other shore he found the Indian tracks where they came out, which he informed the boys. He then instructed them to stay where they were and keep a sharp lookout while he went on down the river to ses if they could get through. He cautiously wended his way some two hundred yards down the river, when sudenly a quick crackling in a thick bunch of bushes not more than twenty steps in his advance made his hair stand up and nearly throw off his hat. In an instant he had his gun ready for service, when a magnificent buck of the blacktail variety bounded up on a point of the mountain and turned his side to him  The temptation was too great, and in the twinkling of an eye the gun was at his shoulder and he fired. The buck bounded high, fell over and rolled down nearly to his feet. He called back, "All right, boys, we have more meat." He quickly put another load in his gun, drew his big hunting knife, that was made expressly for him in San Antonio, at the commencement of the Civil War, and that he had carried through all his scouts, and bled the buck as hunters do.

He then reasoned thus: "The Indians did not pass here today or that buck would not lie down so close to their trail. In fact, I think he could smell their trail two or three days old, and it is a sure thing that he would not lie down where he could smell them."

Being thus assured by practice and experience he moved cheerfully on to the next crossing of the river.

He waded here as at first crossing and found the Indian trail going in and coming out as at the first crossing. Here the bluff receded from the river on the Texas side and the calley opened to a beautiful level. He returned and went back to where Tom and George were very anxiously awaiting him.

He explained his discoveries and they were as eager and ready to go forward as he was, so they mounted their horses and forded the river and went on to where the big buck lay. They dismounted and dressed the buck and prepared one of the pack mules, and lifted him on, head, hornes and all, tied him firmly to the pack saddle, mounted and went forward, crossing the river out on to Texas soil and the beautiful level country and the change of scenery was so inspiring contrasted with the dismal and lonesome passage of the Lower Narrows of the Rio Grande that Tom and George set up the Texas yell of victory that reverbrated from bluff to bluff.

A short distance below the Narrows stands a large cotton wood tree on the Texas side of the river and when our party reached the tree, the place and all surroundings were too inviting for a camping place for the night for Jeff to pass. His experienced eye took in the situation at a glance so he said "Halt, this is too good to pass." As Indian signs had been disagreeably in evidence all the afternoon the experienced frontiersman, as he had been taught so to do utilized every natural advantage that woud tend to ward off the surprise and sudden attack of the enemy in this connection.

It is due the reader to give a brief sketch or pen picture of this almost perfect camp ground for defence. Standing under this grand, old cottonwood tree on the Texas bank looking north and south, a deep, broad pool of water runs north and south. A perpendicular bluff on the west or Mexican side, a high bank on the east until it comes to within 100 yards of the tree, either way, north or south, Here the bank is about five feet high and sets back some twenty feet from the water almost level east from the top of the bank is a beautiful level without rock or shrub but covered with best of grass. Here our little party of three felt like they could stand off every roving Indian on the Rio Grande.

After horses and mules were all attended to and we had gone back to the tree we looked down the river to where the bank set into the water about one hundred yards distance, and there sat a fine wild goose. Tom said it would be cruel and almost a wanton waste for me to shoot that goose, but I wanted to keep up my "rep" as a fine shot, and I said, "Jeff, if you are willing I will shoot its head off, at least thereby giving it a chance for its life." Jeff replied, "Poor goose, I pity its chance." After which Tom raised his gun, took deliberate aim and fired. The goose turned over on its back with its head cut off as smooth as if with an axe. Jeff said, "Tom, if the Indians do charge us I intend to give you the first shot, and see if you can kill Indians like you can geese."

Tom said, "Good, I won't loose my 'rep'."

We moved everything over the bank to the nice little level that extended to the water. Tom brought his goose and we skinned the big buck, and oh, my! He was fat! We then set in to have a night's feast such as no man ever had, and if we could have had a jug of "O. B. Joyful" we would have had the ideal meal. But let me tell you what we did have—we had roasted buck ribs as fine as mortal man ever tasted, roasted goose, roasted cat fish, roasted bread a la ranger style, Rio Grande water, strong coffee and health and West Texas appetites, which is about the biggest thing that wild game ever ran up against. A man may be poor in purse, but in Texas he is rich in health, rich in hospitality, rich in patriotism, rich in bravery, rich in honor and big rich in a broad and expansive appetite for pretty women, red liquor and good eating, and as those three were no exception to the general West Texan, they set in to have a full night of it as far as their stock of good things of West Texas was concerned.

The fire was completely hidden by the river bank, which was just high enough for one to stand up straight and look over the beautiful level where their horses grazed, while the other two kept themselves busy feasting, barbecuing fat buck meat, baking bread and fixing up generally for any emergency that might arise during the furtherance of their journey, as the light of the fire shone plainly on the water a tremendous fish would flounce and make the water boil and whirl, no doubt he was attracted by the smell of the big buck. Jeff said, "Boys, I am going to hook that fellow with my little hook just to see how he feels on a long limber pole."

So suiting the action of the word, he cut a long willow pole, fastened his little hook and line to it, put on a piece of the fried meat and droped it into the water. The fish took it at once and moved slowly off to the other shore. Jeff gave the pole a jerk, and it hooked the fish like it hung in a log, but it steadily moved straight forward and the line was not sufficient to raise his head or turn him in the least, and broke. Jeff sat down and meditated a little; got up and picked up the buck's head, took it near the fire, drew his big knife, and Tom said, "What are you going to do now?" He replied, "I am going to cut off one of these horns, make me a fish hook and catch that fish. The boys laughed, as a matter of course, but he said, "We will see where the laugh comes in the morning." So he deliberately hacked off one of the horns just below the lower prong, and cut off the horn just above the next prong, went and hobbled his horse and brought the stake rope and fastened it securely just below where he had cut off the horn the second time, cut four or five pounds of the meat and wrapped it around the horn, but left the prong uncovered, fastened the bait securely around the horn with a piece of his small line that was left to the pole, tied his rope to a small willow sapling and threw out his bait, saying, "Boys, I will show you how to catch big fish in emergencies." So the next morning Jeff's long experience on the frontier where necessity had to be the mother of invention proved good for he had the big fish, and when he drew him out George remarked: "I'll be d—d if that ain't a whale or the fish that swallowed Jonah, my name ain't George Laird."

They now had fish enough to feed a regiment and could not use a pound of it, so Jeff said, "It is a pity for the vultures to eat this fish. I will take off my bridle bits and brand him and turn him loose in this big water, and as the Indians have stolen many horses and cattle from me should they catch him they will think I have a fish brand as well as a horse and cattle brand." So they branded him thus [Heart-B] and H B and turned him loose. He swam a few feet, turned down his head, threw up his tail and disappeared beneath the Rio Grande waters. They extracted the hook, getting the other piece of the line, and tied the two pieces together, so the line was as good as ever, only for the knot.

As our little party of three had feasted as no other men had, our horses were well rested up, and having plenty of good, barbecued venison and enough bread baked to last them through any emergency they mounted and turned their course for the once famous Hot Springs, on the east side of the river. The old signs and trails leading in to the springs indicated that the Indians held the virtues of these springs as the people of old Biblical times held the Pool of Siloam.

After resting and taking in the surroundings of the springs we mounted our horses and rode up the river some two or three miles Texas side. We rode straight up the valley east of the timber and we came to a fresh trail of ten or fifteen horses going into the river. We stopped, talked and hesitated a little but went straight ahead for probably one mile when we came to another trail just like the first; here we parlied much longer, but Jeff said that he would like to go on and see the whole thing if we could. So we very hesitatingly rode on, Jeff going some little distance in the lead. We had gone but a little distance when Tom rode up to him and said, if we are attacked and we are almost sure to be, you are so big they are sure to kill you." He laughingly replied, "Tom, I don't know just what I will do, but I tell you what I think I will do." They had halted and George rode up. Jeff said, pointing to deep gully that high water had washed out, "if we are attacked in such a place as this we will drive the spurs to our horses and jump them in it, dismount and win the fight. If we are attacked when we have no chance of cover, I will jump off my horse and shoot him through the brain, you and George jump off of your horses, let horses and mules go, and we will all make breastworks of my dead horse and win the fight, for we have got it to do to get back and report this country, and as to their killing me, don't have any fear on that score, for they can't; my guardian angel, or "still small voice" has always told me what, and how to do, and I have always heeded its promptings."

The word promptings had hardly escaped from his lips when the yell of a band of Indians echoed and re-echoed from bluff to bluff all along the Rio Grande caused the hair on our heads to raise straight up, and looking in the direction from which it came, ten Indians some three hundred yards distant were coming on us with the speed of a hurricane. Jeff said, "Leave the mules, drive the spurs to your horses and jump into that gulley." This was done as quick as any mad or desperate leap was ever made by any man or men. The mules were so frightened that they jumped in after, and a clear voice rang out, "Jump off. George hold the horses." The sudden disappearance of the little party caused the Indians to circle, which gave the party time to prepare for action. Jeff said: "They will come around within one hundred and fifty yards or two hundred yards of us to draw our fire, and get our exact location, so Tom, as I promised to give you the first shot, I want you to make it the best of your life, for on our first two shots depends defeat or victory. When they come around to draw our fire I want you to kill the lead Indian, and I will kill the next one, and George, you hold the horses, and don't shoot unless Tom and I fail to check them, and they come right on to us. Then let loose the horses and shoot to kill." By this time Tom's nerves seemed to be as unruffled as a May morning and a smile of determination, so plainly depicted on his countenance, such as the beholder could never forget.

The Indians circled and came around within one hundred and fifty yards at full speed when "pop," "pop" went Tom's and Jeff's guns, and the lead Indian fell back and his horse jumped from under him. The second one's horse bounded high over the fallen one just as Jeff pulled the trigger, which brought him above the sight, and the ball killed his horse; the Indian struck the ground runruning with the speed of a deer until he clutched his hand in the mane of the fallen Indian's horse, bounded upon his back, and then circled and rode at full speed to an elevation some half mile distant and halted. They could be seen plainly by our little party, but the high bank of the providential gully at the same time hid us from the Indians. The bottom of the gully was comparatively level, so Jeff said, "Lead your horses, the mules will follow. We must take time by the forelock, and get out of here before they get reinforcements and find where we are. We led our horses a short distance down the gully where a small elevation hid the Indians, and here we mounted our horses and Jeff said, "We will ride for all our horses have got in them until we strike the foot hills, the mules will follow; which they did, and for some ten miles we did some wild and daring riding, until they struck the foot hill, coming on to a nice spot of grass and a nice, little round mound near by. Jeff said, "Halt! We must rest and graze our horses a while as they have done us noble and never to be forgotten service in the last hour."

We did not unsaddle or unpack, but took the bits out of the horses' mouths, so that they could eat grass without hindrance. We had plenty of barbecued venison that had been prepared for this or any other emergency, and were preparing to appease our hunger, when we looked back from whence we came, and one, two, three signal smokes shot up high above the muntains.

Jeff said: "See there, boys; there are three parties of them, and they are signaling to get together and surround us in that gully. I will take me a hunk of meat and bread and go up on that little hill and watch, while you watch the horses." This was done for one hour, when we mounted and struck out for Carizo Pass station, via Eagle Springs. We reached the springs late in the evening, watered our almost famished horses, filled our canteens and moved on to find a suitable place to camp after dark in case the Indians should follow us. We found a suitable place to camp, ate a hearty lunch, spread down our blankets and slept as soundly as though nothing unusual had happened during the day. The next morning they awoke rather late, but were fully refreshed and as gay as larks. Carizo Pass station plain in view, we made a pot of Western strong coffee, and with barbecued buck and that same old appetite, had an enjoyable breakfast, after which we packed up and went on to the station, our heads set homeward. We reached the station and prepared to board the first eastbound train, not forgetting to return the lady her little fish hook, with many thanks, saying, "Madam, you ought to keep that hook and line for a show, for it caught a catfish that would weigh over one hundred pounds," which was the truth, but it did not pull him out.

The train came and everything was loaded, and our little party, as the train pulled out, took their seats to quietly think over their trip on the Rio Grande. After some little time Tom and George said: "Jeff, we don't know whether to tell that fish story or not. To a heap of people it will look mighty fishy." He said: "Yes, but nevertheless it is a fact that all experienced fishermen who have caught big catfish know that often a hook is set out and a small catfish twelve or fifteen inches long gets fast on the hook, and a big catfish comes along and swallows the little one, and the fisherman gets them both; and the hook never sticks in the big fish's mouth. The lack of experience will make the story fishy, that's all."

In due time we reached Baird and called on Mr. Clebe Merchant and made an unfavorable report on the glowing prospects of the last big ranch that might be obtained on Texas and Mexico soil jointly.

The report was that the river did not run continuously only for a few months in the year, but stood in pools; that the cattle would cross over and stray back for miles into Mexico, where they would be an easy prey to the Mexican and other cattle thieves in general, and that the drain on the herds would be greater than the increase.

So the brilliant hopes of the big cattle ranch of T. B. Hardley and Clabe Merchant on the Rio Grande was abandoned in proof that their judgment was good.

Some time afterwards a young man, full of life, vigor and enterprise, discovered the location of the big cottonwood tree that has been described in this recital. He married him a noble, pretty wife, full of hope, courage and devotion. They loaded their effects, with lumber fixtures and a mechanic to build them a house, and a boat to ride upon the waters of this big pool. Here they located under this big cottonwood tree, built them a house, and were monarchs of all they surveyed for a time, until a band of murderers came upon them and murdered them, cutting off her fair and beautiful head with an axe, robbing the house of such things as they wanted, loaded them into their boat, landed the boat over on the Mexican shore, and have never been heard of since.

Later, Sam Cutbirth and the McWhorter Brothers, Winfield Scott and others moved their herds to that section, and the drain on their herds, as our little party wisely predicted, was so great that their ranches were abandoned.

## A Letter From Capt. Maltby.

Admiral, Texas, Dec. 17, 1904.

Mr. N. C. Bawcom, Sweetwater, Texas: My Dear Sir—As this is my birthday, at which I arrive at my seventy-fifth mile-post on life's journey, and as it was your lot to be in the right place at the proper time to render me valuable service, as may yet be demonstrated in the near future. Your letter of recent date earnestly asking a brief statement of my long residence on the frontier of Texas, my scouting and trailing of Indians, with the personal knowledge of the losses of cattle and horses by the Comanche and Kiowa tribes of Indians, and not recovered by their rightful owners, received. Up to the present time I have strenuously refused to make such a statement as I now am going to make to you. My reasons for not wishing to convey the information are on account of my advanced age and enfeebled condition, and, in fact, not having the courage or disposition to charge for my time in going long distances to give testimony in the cases of losses by Indian depredations. My time, age, aches and pains are about all that I have left. Added to these, an invalid family makes up the sum total of my heritage, after spending my youth, strength, vigor and manhood in defense, both of our National and State Governments.

My life and career as a frontiersman of Texas dates back to 1850, and extends over the period of time that dates down to 1874, both dates inclusive—that is to say, that I commenced an active frontier life early in 1850 and closed my activities with the ending of the year 1874. I believe I commanded either State Rangers or minute men during as a great a period as any man living at the present, or perhaps, as ever did live in Texas. I believe that I made as many scouts and followed as many Indian trails as any man that is living on the frontier at the present time or in the past within the memory of man.

In the year of 1850 I was employed by the United States Government in locating, building and hauling supplies to many of the Government posts, or forts, namely, Fort Worth, in Tarrant county; Fort Belknap, in Young county; Fort Phantom Hill, in Jones county; Fort Mason, in Mason county; Fort Clark, in Kinney county; Camp Colorado, in Coleman county, and also Fort Concho, in Tom Green county, the latter fort being established in 1867. I worked in the different capacities of teamster, wagon-master, carpenter, scout, dispatcher, and, like David Copperfield, "doer of odd jobs."

In June, 1858, I got married and settled in Burnet county, and engaged in stock raising. In July of that year the settlers in that section of country were called upon to meet at Dr. Wilson Barton's ranch for the purpose of organizing for protection against the raids of murderous redskins, at that time wards of the National Government. The meeting was fairly well attended, and a company of minute men was organized and the work of trying to protect the women, children and our property was instituted. I was elected as one of the officers of this company, and we made monthly scouts during the year of 1858, and the organization was maintained until the fall of 1859. In the spring of 1861 the Indians began making monthly raids on the frontier, particularly in Burnet county, and especially in our immediate neighborhood, and it began to look as though they would steal all the work stock as well as other horses in the county. One of our neighbors, Walford Johnson, came and asked me to assist in getting every man living within a reasonable distance of our homes to meet at the place of Benjamin Owens, a wealthy old bachelor, for the purpose of organizing another minute company as the only means of protection. At that time a great many men had volunteered and gone into the Confederate service, but the call was promptly responded to, and at the appointed place and on the designated date every man in that section, old or young, ministers of the gospel and boys under the age required for military duty attended and were enlisted in a regularly organized military company The men who were too old to scout were assigned the task of supplying the sinews of war, such as money, provisions, animals, guns, ammunition and other things necessary to carry out the plans and designs of a well-equipped organization; and all boys old enough to ride and shoot were required to scout the country and notify the command of any Indians seen or freshly-made Indian trails discovered. The command of this company was forced upon me because of my years of experience and long service with the United States Government. The company was not organized any too soon, for it was but a few days later when the Indians came into that neighborhood and stole all the work and saddle horses that were in the lots and stables, and before we could follow them we had to go on the range and get horses to ride. This delay left us but little chance to catch them, but as we wanted to learn the trails they traveled, we followed them about ninety miles to a crossing on the San Saba river, and learned from the people in that section that in 1859 the Indians had driven thirteen herds of cattle and horses across the river at that point.

We returned from this trip, having accomplished nothing more than to obtain the information in regard to the route they had traveled. On the next light of the moon the Indians made another raid into the same neighborhood and killed Walford Johnson, the man who had assisted me in getting up the company. They had also murdered Mrs. Johnson and her little daughter, about four or five years old. This murder was committed on Dog branch, about one mile from my home, and at the same place from where the Indians afterwards drove off about three hundred head of my cattle and sixteen head of stock horses and one stallion. I got the news of the killing of the Johnson family late in the evening of the day on which it occurred. I had been riding very hard all day, gathering my horses to drive them to Caldwell county, south of Austin, hoping in this way to save at least a few of them. I reached home about sundown, and had just eaten my supper when my first lieutenant, John Owens, rode up and informed me of the killing of the Johnson family. I had just put my horses in a pasture, for which the Indians were doubtless headed, but before reaching it they met and brutally murdered Johnson and his family, and by this incident saved to me my horses. John Owens, Alex Burton and myself rode all night getting the company together, and early the next morning had collected thirty men, old and young, after which I was one of the first to reach the tragic spot. We heard a noise in a thicket, and on investigating found Mrs. Johnson's one-year-old baby boy with an arrow shot through his arm. The little fellow had certainly suffered inexpressible agony, lying there for hours wounded, fevered, thirsty, without nourishment or a particle of human attention; but even the wild animals prowling the forests of that desolate, rugged, mountainous country had been more merciful than the redskin demons, and had satiated their hunger with other prey than a wounded babe, crying in the dark for a dead mother. When attacked, Mrs. Johnson had doubtless run her horse near a dogwood thicket in which the child was found, and with a mother's love, last kiss and farewell prayer, had thrown her child into the brush.

When we assembled my horse was completely exhausted, for I had ridden him fully eighty miles in the last twenty-four hours, and nothing but a Texas horse of the best mettle could have stood the ordeal. An old gentleman by the name of Baker, who was too old to scout, offered me the use of his horse. His offer was gladly accepted, our saddles were changed and, mounting the fresh horse, I called for all who could ride ninety miles without resting to follow me. Fifteen of the thirty men volunteered, and as news had been brought to me that the Indians had been seen that morning traveling in a northwesterly direction, the direction in which they had always left our community, I naturally concluded that they would cross the San Saba river at their old and well-known crossing place, and to that point I took the nearest and most direct route, not trying to follow their trail, but anticipating that we could beat them to the crossing and there lie in wait for them; but my calculations were wrong and our efforts came to naught. After going to the north line of Burnet county the Indians had turned back to the south line of that county, and thence northwest through Llano county, where they killed two men who were plowing in a field. They then went west and crossed the San Saba river about six miles above their usual crossing place, and at a place where they had never before been known to cross, and this was four days after we had reached the river at the point where we expected to trap them. And in this connection permit me to say that, after my many years of experience, from 1850 to 1874, and many sad disappointments in trying to out-general the Indians, that if God or a special providence ever protected any race or races of people, it certainly was the Comanche and Kiowa Indians. I could enumerate numerous instances in substantiation of this conclusion, but suffice it to ask what human intellect or animal instinct could have so accurately divined the designs of the white men and enabled the Indian to thwart every plan laid for his capture, and to only bring on an engagement when all was in his favor. Even a handful of them, confined on a reservation, and presumably unarmed, could defy the world's greatest Government, break away from all restraint, going into a virtually defenseless country, murdering, plundering, robbing and terrorizing fearless men, escaping vengeance and returning at leisure to their reservations.

In the year 1867, G. C. Arnett and myself went on a cow hunt, and established our first camp near old Uncle Jimmy Boyce's, who had good stock pens, and was then living on the North San Gabriel, in the northern portion of Burnet county. In our party there were the following resident citizens: E. P. Boyce, William Skaggs, Marcus Skaggs, Millard Moreland, Thomas Wolf, James Sims, S. S. Johnston and Josiah C. Bawcom. I acted as cook, but always on cow hunts of this kind in that section of the country I took with me my saddle, a good saddle horse and the best firearms I had, as did all the other members of our party, as we were liable to meet hostile Comanche or Kiowa Indians at any time, these being the only hostile Indians that ever came into our section of country in-so-far as my personal knowledge extends.

These were the most trying times that I ever experienced in frontier life. People may talk of times that tried men's souls, but if men were ever put to a more crucial test than were the frontiersmen of Texas, I cannot comprehend by what miraculous agency they stood the ordeal. At that time no man's life was safe, and he knew not at what hour his family or friends might be murdered, tortured or, even worse than either, taken captives by the Indians. It was simply one long, dreadful vigil, fear and apprehension. Had it been so that the citizens could have followed the Indians to the utmost confines of the United States and inflicted upon them deserved and effective punishment, it would have taken but a reasonable length of time to dispose of the Indian question, but such was not the case. They would slip away from the reservations, do their murdering and stealing, and unless overtaken within a few hours they would have a sufficient start and advantage to reach the reservation from whence they came and there be safe from molestation by the outraged citizens and immune from punishment by the Government, for the citizen could go no further than the resrvation, and after doing his devilment the Indian made it a special point to get there first, and of course there was no way for the Government or injured citizens to identify any particular Indians as the guilty parties; hence no punishment could be legally inflicted.

The next morning after establishing our camp, G. C. Arnett, Joe Bawcom, William Skaggs, E. P. Boyce and S. S. Johnson went west to a place on Morgan's creek where there were some big cedar brakes and glades covered with good green grass, and here horses and cattle were nearly always found grazing, and it was one of the worst Indian haunts in that entire section of country. As Arnett and his men advanced cautiously around a cedar-covered point, they discovered a party of Indians not far from them. The Indians were leading several horses, and one of them was riding a splendid pony, which the men readily recognized as my property, a kind of pet which I called Belle. Arnett and his party did not feel safe in attacking the Indians, but made a dash for camp and arrived late in the evening, their horses almost exhausted. We immediately began making preparations to start after the Indians early the next morning, which we did, leaving Mr. Sims in charge of the camp, while I was placed in command of the squad. On reaching the place where the Indians had been seen the day before we discovered that they had evidently been frightened themselves, as their trail showed that for a distance of ten or fifteen miles they had ridden as fast as possible, leading several horses.

The trail led north up to and along the east line of San Saba county; then it turned east to the north part of Hamilton county. Along the trail we frequently saw signs where they had roped horses. In fact, they had captured every horse along the line of their retreat, and every one of them was leading about two horses. Near the north line of Hamilton county the Indian trail intercepted and followed a large cattle trail. We followed this trail only a few miles further and found that another Indian trail came into the cattle trail, the last Indians coming from the East, and this squad seemed to have been about equal in numbers to the squad we were following; and they had also been leading a considerable number of horses, a fact which we determined because the horses were travling three in a bunch, showing that one horse was being ridden and two others led. We also found along the big trail where they had killed three or four young beeves.

From all indications, the Indians would have easily outnumbered us five to one, and, besides, they had plenty of good, fresh horses and several hours the start, while our horses were tired out. So we held a consultation and decided that it would be foolish to continue the pursuit any further, as the prospects were that we could not overtake the Indians, and the probabilities were that we would get the worst of an encounter with them should one take place. We then went west to the San Saba river, and then down the Colorado river, through the cedar brakes of Morgan's creek, to where we first strucĸ the trail, and then back to our camp, where we found Mr. Sims, who had carefully attended to everything during our absence. We then resumed the work of gathering cattle pending another redskin disturbance from some Indian reservation.

I will say that it was a notorious fact that the people of Hamilton county lost a great many horses and cattle about this time. We did not learn who lost the big herd, the trail of which we struck in the northern part of Hamilton county, as we neither saw horses nor men along the route we traveled; but I afterwards learned that the principal losers were James Carter, "Big Bill" Keith and Solomon Barron, and others whose names I do not now recall, as that was so many years ago.

As to parties who lost horses and cattle, and who have good and just claims, I cannot remember all of them at this time, but will enumerate the following, all of whom I think can, or at least should, recover:

The Northington family of Lampasas county; John Hinton of Llano county; Ewin Lacy's widow, of Burnet county, and Joe Bawcom, of McCuloch county.

But, in conclusion, I certainly know, but cannot prove positively, the identity of the tribes of Indians that committed the depredations in all of the counties from Kinney on the west to Tarrant on the east, and north and south across the State from 1850 to 1874. These depredations were committed, encouraged or guided by the Indians held, fed and protected by the United States Government, and known as Penatocas, or Southern Comanches, and only differing from the Northern Comanches in complexion, stature and general make-up, as the white men of the North differ from the white men of the

South. I have at different times been on the reservations of the Penatocas, have been in camp with two thousand of the Northern Comanches, have seen many Indians pursued and killed while making their raids on the unprotected frontier, and all that I have seen I unequivocally pronounce as wards of the Government, even their trappings and fixtures fully verifying this conclusion, for I have observed closely and have arrived at this conclusion impartially and because facts would warrant no other conclusion in the matter.

There were many who lost both cattle and horses in the big raid on the San Saba river. Some of these parties lost very heavily. As to small losses, I could name very many of them, the owners of which are justly entitled to recover for their property; but the long lapse of time and the disappearance of witnesses, by death and otherwise, added to the necessary delay of the courts, makes a small claim utterly worthless. As to your question about attorneys in this class of cases, I would recommend Col. I. R. Hitt and Wm. H. Robeson, Bond Building, Washington, D. C., as they are perfectly reliable and possess extraordinary ability. In your letter you ask the question positively, if I am personally knowing of any big bands of Indians that came down on the frontier people, and, if so, what counties did they raid? My answer is, Yes; the Indians that I, G. C. Arnett, Joe Bawcom and others followed out of Burnet county into Hamilton county were a part of a big band of Indians, as the trail proved to concentrate with other trails and made a very large trail.

A band of one hundred or more went, all in a body, into Coleman county.

The big raid on the San Saba must have contained several hundred Indians, as they swept the range of all stock in their track.

The last raid in 1874, in Coleman county, where I struck with my company of State Rangers and completely routed them, horse and foot, each division in detail, after they had formed in several divisions for the purpose of stealing horses, when they came together to spread over a large section of country and drive everything in the way of cattle and horses. To show how completely I and my company defeated their hellish purposes and schemes of murder and robbery, they were completely whipped, discouraged and left the country without getting a single hoof of cattle or horses, only what they killed and ate, and from that time down to the present date they have never returned.

For your satisfaction and pleasure, whom I hold in the highest esteem, I would go into the details of this subject more fully and write an account of all the horrors it has been my misfortune to witness during my long frontier life were my physical ability such as would permit of the labor. I have not told one-half of the incidents of horrors and outrages that I have personally witnessed and experienced.

Fraternally yours,     W. J. MALTBY.

# BOOK III.

# Newspaper Extracts.

Extract from the Southern Mercury, Dallas, Texas, of October 31, 1903:

The county exhibits were all good. Taylor county carried off the blue ribbon. In Callahan county, though there was the finest individual exhibits to be seen, the vegetables of this collection far excelled in size those shown in other counties. The exhibition here of Mr. W. J. Maltby, is an illustration of what has been, and what can be accomplished within a few short years. This enterprising gentleman had on exhibition all grains, every species of fruit (and I believe about as many vegetables), that were exhibited at this fair. The vegetables he had on exhibition far exceeded in size those seen elsewhere, as one can judge by the following: One roasting ear (perhaps the largest ever grown) measured 4 inches in diameter, 12 inches in circumference, and the length of a large Mason jar, after two or three inches had been cut off. A "Mammoth Chile" squash, weighed 103 pounds. Mr. Maltby informed me these were grown principally for stock, on account of the immensity of size, though they were as nice for table use as the ordinary pumpkin. Then he had the William Henry Mall Price prize-taker (I am not certain if this is correct) onion, grown from seed sown in February, that attained a size of something a little less than two pounds. Two "Golden Queen" pepper pods took the blue ribbon at Abilene Fair, as did also his ochra. The pods were as large as a quince or a pear. He had the best flavored sun dried fruit, apples, peaches, Mission grapes and tomatoes, too, were sun dried. These Mission grapes are indigenous to Mexico, where they have been growing for hundreds of years. Mr. Maltby went to Mexico for them, says they do well in his country. Dried, they are nearly as good as the California raisin.

Dried tomatoes were something new to me; the flavor was good, and one need never be at a loss in winter time to know how to make good soup. The yellow preserve tomato about the size of a walnut was the kind seen. I asked him in regard to his almond crop, seeing some. The yield is uncertain, or has proven so with him thus far, though as his trees get older he hopes for better results; says it is a lovely tree. In this same collection was to be found sugar made of sorghum, and as far as I was capable of judging, it compared very favorably with that used in her family that sells nine pounds to the dollar. Syrup made of the sorghum was a bright golden color. I was tempted to taste it, but had tasted so much I doubted my ability to pass judgment. There were thirty-four varieties of wood on exhibition, thirty-three of which were grown by the exhibitor. The one not his was a pecan. Now, readers, this has all been accomplished in the miraculously short time of twelve years by Mr. Maltby, and in justice to him, and myself as well, I will say that Mr. M. has possessed advantages over us. He has availed himself of travel, and has no doubt profited by the experience of observation, while we, less fortunate, have to experiment for ourselves and let "chill penury repress our noble rage" in trying to emulate the example of our more successful neighbor. "STAR."

Baird Star, Baird, Texas, March 16, 1905:

Editor Star: To give Mrs. Joel Nabers a more correct account of the location of the historical government post of Phantom Hill, and to refresh the memory of Mr. Jesse Johnson, Sr., in Comanche Chief, I herewith give you the facts in detail as near as the memory of man can narrate after the lapse of fifty-five years; and in this connection will give your many readers the dates of the location of most of the government posts in Texas, by whom located, etc., as a matter of history that should be of interest to the many who have enjoyed the blessings that have followed their location.

From 1844 to 1852 General Arbuckle, of the United States army, was in command of the western part of Arkansas, the Indian Nations, with their five tribes, and the northern part of Texas, with his headquarters at Fort Smith, Ark. After the close of the Mexican war of 1846-7, the United States was responsible for the protection of Texas, with a frontier on the north on the 32nd parallel running from Red river to the Rio Grande, a distance of six or seven hundred miles. This country was roamed over and depredated upon by all the different hostile bands of Indians, and from El Paso on the west to Corpus Christi on the south, a like distance of seven hundred miles. there was exposure to the depredations of marauding bands of Mexicans that infested the borders all along the Rio Grande.

So our Uncle Samuel had fifteen hundred miles of much exposed frontier to guard, and the only way to do it was to build a line of posts from east to west and north to south, with many intermediate posts near the settlements to guard the settlers and their property. General Twiggs was placed in command of the west or Rio Grande division, with headquarters at San Antonio, and ordered the building of the following posts, to-wit: Fort Bliss, El Paso; Fort Leaton. Presidio Del Norte; Fort Duncan, Eagle Pass; Fort McIntosh, Laredo; Fort Brown, Brownsville.

As it will be only necessary to mention one of these named posts and Robert E. Lee's connection with it, we go back and take up the thread of our narrative in the location of Phantom Hill and what led up to it.

In 1849 General Arbuckle ordered the fitting out of an expedition of one company of United States infantry, Captain Marcellus French to command, Lieutenant Myers to act as quartermaster, with one hundred ox and mule teams, carpenters, sappers and miners, and everything necessary to build and maintain a government post in the Creek Nation, somewhere near the Canadian river. I employed myself to the then acting quartermaster at Fort Smith, Captain Montgomery by name and rank. He kept me in his office while the expedition was fitting out to carry orders and purchase what the department did not have in stock, and when the expedition started I was sent along as a supernumerary to do anything, or to work in such harness as the quartermaster might throw on me.

The progress of the expedition was rather slow as we had to make the road as we went. When we had got say seventy-five miles from Fort Smith and had to stop to build a road over a creek with high banks, one of the men was taken sick and on the third day developed a full case of the smallpox of a malignant type. Here was consternation of the worst form, and the only thing that could be done for the government doctor to order every man up to his tent and vaccinate as fast as possible. The sick man died and no one else of the entire party took the disease. Considering this in all its bearings, it was Providential.

The expedition moved on to its objective point, and Fort Arbuckle, No. 1, was located and built. When built it looked more like an old-fashioned nigger's quarter than a government post, for there was nothing to be had but the native timber as it stood in the forest.

Late in the fall Captain French discovered a better location for a post, some eighteen miles south at a big spring near the Washita river, in the Chickasaw Nation. So Fort Arbuckle, No. 1, was given to Black Beaver, chief of the Delaware tribe of Indians for his headquarters, and the troops were moved to the Big Wild Horse Spring in the Chickasaw Nation, and Fort Arbuckle, No. 2, built, where it has stood as a government post ever since.

A big government ox train loaded with supplies arrived about the first of November. I went back to Fort Smith with it and reached there the last of the month. A cabin was built in the Porto river bottom, a big canebrake, and the oxen were moved to it. I was put in charge with a few of the teamsters to herd the oxen, preparatory to the location of two government posts on or about the

32nd parallel in Texas, which posts were named Belknap and Phantom Hill, respectively.

So in the spring of 1850 a train of 100 or 150 ox and six-mule teams was fitted out at Fort Smith, with several companies of the Fifth Infantry, and ordered forward to locate the above posts. When the expedition reached old Fort Washington in the Choctaw Nation, near the line Texas, Lieutenant Bliss was ordered to take some men and teams and go to Shreveport, La., after some ordnance stores, etc., with instructions to travel back on the west side of Red river until he struck the road made by the command which was to cross Red river at Coffey's Bend at a little town called Preston, and establish a quartermaster's store there, with Major George W. Wood as quartermaster.

I was sent with Lieutenant Bliss to Shreveport, at which place I was promoted to engineer. With six fine gray government mules and a six-pound brass cannon I was to head the expedition the balance of the trip. To say that I was proud of my promotion would be expressing it very mildly.

In the country through which we traveled the settlements were few and far between, but coming to a nice farm house where everything betokened some refinement, Lieutenant Bliss ordered me to halt while he dismounted and went in. He presently reappeared with a nice old lady and, oh, my! two beautiful daughters, for us boys to feast our eyes upon, which was a treat indeed, for we had been away from home and society until the pretty girls looked to us like angels. The old lady was much excited over the cannon, and inquired of the Lieutenant if it was the kind of gun that Captain Taylor had in Mexico. The Lieutenant smilingly replied, "Yes, madam, this is one of the little things General Taylor had for toys when he played with the Mexicans."

Lieutenant Bliss struck the road made by the command in Grayson County west of Preston and followed it, overtaking the command where it had halted and located Fort Belknap, Post No.1. Here a rest of some time was taken to recruit the teams for the onward march to locate Post No. 2. So I will say that about the 15th of December the order was given to load, hitch up and march, and my recollection is, with one company of the Fifth Infantry, Major Thomas as the commanding officer, Black Beaver, chief of the Delaware Indians, as guide, and 100 mule and ox teams to haul camp equippage and supplies. The expedition moved forward on Captain Marcy's Santa Fe trail, which led west on the north side of the Clear Fork of the Brazos.

The third night after leaving Fort Belknap we camped in a beautiful basin surrounded by mountains, an ideal camp ground, and as we had to depend entirely on grass for forage, the mules were tied to the wagons until 2 o'clock in the morning and then turned loose to graze, with men to herd till daylight.

· This was my morning to go on herd. My mess consisted of three, myself and two others. About four o'clock my mess called me to breakfast. I had no appetite that morning which was unusual for me, as I was known as a good feeder. When day began to break orders sounded to drive up and hitch up, at which time the aged chief, Black Beaver, with his experience of West Texas, went to Major Thomas and told him that he had better stay at that ideal camp ground, as there was a fearful "Norther" approaching, to which Major Thomas turned a deaf ear, as he had a fine closed hack and a fine pair of black horses to draw it. By good daylight Major Thomas, guide and soldiers had taken the old Marcy trail and gone, giving the quartermaster notice when he was to leave. It was the supposition that the Major's hack tracks would plainly mark the way; but, alas!,the supposition proved wrong; for a few moments after the quartermaster left camp, myself with the cannon, the caisson and the major's baggage wagon following close up to him, the storm broke upon us with all its fury; and when the quartermaster reached the place where he thought he had been directed to turn off from the Marcy trail and travel in a westerly direction he turned off, but could not find any marks of the Major's hack tracks.

I followed close up to the quartermaster with the caisson and the

Major's baggage wagon close up to me. When the quartermaster found himself, the storm had drifted him some three miles south of the trail to a big canyon that we could not cross. There was but one way out of this distressing dilemma, and that was to turn back and face the storm of sleet and hail, that seemed to strike us with as much force as if shot out of a cannon.

By a superhuman effort the quartermaster drove the spurs into his horse and held him to the wagon tracks that we had made, which brought us back to where we had left the old trail. It required all the energy that we drivers could put forth to run along by the side of our teams and force them against the storm, which struck them and us full in the face.

When we had got back to where we had left the trail the quartermaster said, "Boys, for God sake, try to make a fire, for I believe we shall all freeze to death." And then the language he used about his commanding officer for not leaving a guide to direct him, would not do to put in print. There was an ax in the Major's baggage wagon and some dry material. John White, the driver, got them out, and as there was plenty of dry mesquite trees at the spot, I took the ax and went to splitting up wood with a will, urged on by necessity. The two other drivers kindled a fire, and in a short time we had a life-giving blaze. The drivers brought up their wagons, jumped off their saddle mules and hovered over the fire.

During this time the quartermaster had never stopped his mad ride in search of the Major's hack tracks. I heard a halloa. I threw down the ax. My team was nearby, standing all huddled up, freezing to death. I grabbed my lines and whip and forced them to their utmost, running along side of them, and soon overtook the quartermaster and kept up with him on a run until we reached Camp Necessity.

And why Necessity?

The Major's fine horses stopped and refused to go any further. and he had to stop just where he was; and when he was asked why he had camped in such a place he replied, "It was a military necessity."

Could he have forced his horse a few miles further, the quartermaster and several more men and mules would have fallen victims to his rashness in not heeding the advice of the old Indian.

The soldiers had managed to have good fires. When we reached them the quartermaster was frozen so that he could not dismount and had to be lifted from his horse and carried to the fire. The doctor administered brandy to him and had him rubbed, and his life was saved; but to this day I cannot see how any man could live in the saddle and cover as many miles as he did on that never-to-be-forgotten day.

Some one or two hours later the wagons began to come into camp until twenty or thirty came in; and as the wagonmaster was still back and no one to give orders what to do with the mules, the drivers unharnessed and let them go as they pleased. Late in the day some of the teamsters brought in their teams and left their wagons on the way; and many that had their blankets in the wagons turned their mules loose, got into their wagons, covered up heads and ears and remained so until we went back the next day and halloaed them up. As the mules had been turned loose as they came into camp, they drifted away with the storm. As there was no wagonmaster to give orders, I asked one of the teamsters by the name of Bill Stevens, a very powerful young man, to go with me and see if we could not drive them back. He said yes, and we struck out to herd the mules back. We got off some three miles from camp, running and working, but could not do anything with them, so we had to give them up, and started back to camp, as we supposed. We had not gone far after leaving the mules, when, to our good luck, we met Black Beaver, the guide. He said, "Halloa, Beaver, where are you going?" He said he was going to camp. We said, "Oh, no, Beaver, that ain't the way to camp," which seemed to nettle him—for us to presume to question him in direction and he the guide. He replied, "You go that way, me go this way," and made off and didn't look back. We consulted a few moments, and thought it best to follow Beaver, which saved our lives, for we were surely lost and could not have survived through the night.

About the time myself and Stevens got back to camp three or four of the teamsters came in, bringing their saddle-mules, having turned the rest loose, and had left their wagons. They reported that James Morehead, who had started with them, had not come up and they feared he would freeze to death, whereupon Billy Benton, a noble-hearted boy and a nephew of Senator Benton of Missouri, said to the wagonmaster, William Locklin, "If you will let me have your horse, I will go back and try to get Morehead to camp." The wagonmaster consented but advised him not to go, and others endeavored to dissuade him, but the noble-hearted boy replied, "Morehead shall not freeze to death if I can save him." So he mounted the horse, which was a good one, and he forced him to his best for five miles. He found Morehead sitting down, speechless. He dismounted and tried to lift him on the horse, but he could not do it. So he remounted and returned to camp and reported, as here written. Mr. Locklin called for volunteers to go after Morehead. I responded and also William Kemper and William Lace. So we three caught the first four mules that we came to, hitched them to an unloaded wagon, put a camp kettle full of good solid coals of fire in it, the wagonmaster got a bottle of brandy from the doctor, Kemper got on the saddle mule, Lacey got in the wagon by the kettle of coals and I led the head mule by the bridle. This was our only chance to rescue our comrade, without a trained saddle mule or leader. On reaching the spot designated by Benton we found the poor fellow lying straight on his back. The wagonmaster ran his hand under his clothes and felt of his heart, and said, "Boys, his heart is still." He opened his mouth and poured some brandy down his throat. We then picked him gently up and put him in the wagon, with his feet to the kettle of coals, and went back to camp as we had come, me leading the head mule all the way both ways. We got back about 12 o'clock at night, and here some friendly hand gave me a cup of good, strong coffee, the only thing I had taken since the morning before. Reader, the exhilerating effects of that coffee can't be described. Suffice it to say that it warmed, vibrated and tingled to the ends of my toes, for I had then run and walked in that biting storm over forty miles without food. After drinking that seemingly life-giving coffee, I stood around the fire until I was dry and warm. I then looked around and found a wagon with but one occupant, covered up snug and warm. I quickly crawled in beside him, raised the blankets, snuggled close up to him, with my boots and clothes all on, and was soon in the land of dreams, surrounded by singing birds, flowing fountains and perpetual roses, as a reward for what I had just gone through.

Providence seemed to pity our forlorn condition and sent us a change in the weather, for the next morning the wind had ceased and the sun rose bright and clear. We were all up early, trying to find something to appease the cravings of hunger for by this time the inner man was calling for help in no uncertain feeling. We russled up some fat pickled pork, soldier hard tack and coffee, of which I ate about one pound of raw, fat pork, five or six hard tacks and drank a quart of strong coffee, and then felt equal to any or all emergencies. The wagonmasters were compelled to keep their horses tied up to go in pursuit of the mules; so after we had eaten our hasty and short ration breakfast all struck out, horse and foot, in every direction to round them up. By 10 o'clock we had most of the live mules caught, but many had been frozen and rounded up for the last time by the storm.

Teams were fitted up and we went back to bring up the wagons and men that were left behind in the storm. We found all the men that had been left in their wagons, covered up head and ears in their blankets. By night we had got everything to camp. Rations were issued, we got another square meal, and buried our dead comrade, who, like many thousands, had lost his life in trying to carry out an unnecessary military order.

The next morning what teams were left were hitched to the wagons and Camp Necessity was left. About noon we reached the Clear Fork of the Brazos at a good natural ford, due to the guideship of Black Beaver. The major drove over and I followed him with my cannon. When he reached the rise on the south bank about one mile southwest, a beautiful hill covered with beautiful trees was plain in sight. We moved forward to it, and as we approached it the hill and trees became less and less. When the Major got near it, he halted, called his officers, got out of his hack, and they, with Black Beaver, walked all over the little hill and grove, and when he returned he said, "Here we locate Fort Phantom Hill, for this is one spot where distance lends enchantment to the view." Hence the name, Phantom Hill.

The order was then to drive up and unload, camp and rest. The word "Rest" was like pouring oil of gladness on troubled waters, for we had traveled under the burning suns of summer and in the frosts of winter, since early spring, before we reached this haven.

As the range was as fine as any in the world, and it was necessary to recruit the mules before starting on the long trip back to Fort Smith in the midst of winter, Phantom Hill was an ideal spot for the purpose. Grass and water were abundant for the mules and wild game for the men. There was a heavy crop of acorns in the big rough near the post, and deer and turkeys had collected to it from far and near. They had never heard the report of a gun or seen a white man. They were so fat and contented that they did not seem to fear us, and all we had to do was to sally forth after dark, armed with a long pole, and knock off the low, spreading elms the nice, fat turkeys which we would carry to camp. So we had turkey fixings and flour doings to our heart's content. Antelope were in all directions, 500 in a herd, like flocks of sheep. We thanked the gods of Phantom Hill for giving us this feast, rest and sunshine after the storm. Who can blame the Indians for fighting for this paradise when civilization sought to take it away from them by force of arms?

As my recollection serves me, about the first of January, Mr. Locklin, the wagonmaster, was ordered to hitch up the train and draw rations to carry the outfit back to Preston and at Preston to draw rations to last to Fort Smith.

Everyhing went smooth with us till we got to Preston. Here

Major Wood, the quartermaster, kept several of the best teams, mine with the others. The other boys who had to give up their teams took it as a matter of course. Not so with me. Mine was the fanciest and best team in the train, and I loved them better than I ever loved any mules that were really mine. They turned over to me an old, broken-down team to drive to Fort Smith, and I swore straight up and down that I would not drive them. But as my home and dear mother were at Fort Smith, and the thoughts of getting to see her soon by driving the team, and getting to tell her that her boy had seen the elephant, rhinoceros or some other big animal in the location of Phantom Hill, made me relent; so I made a virtue of necessity, got some shears, roached them up nicely and tied two of the poorest ones behind the wagon. The quartermaster bought corn all through the nations. I fed and curried them and tried to make them look pretty, especially to drive into Fort Smith. So the morning we drove in I hitched them all up, and when we got near the Fort Mr. Locklin halted the train and sent for me.

"Jeff," he said, pointing to his baggage team in the lead, "this is your team to drive into the fort."

Reader, I was prouder of that promotion than any promotion that I ever received in a long life on the frontier of Texas. I hope the reader will pardon this seeming piece of egotism. The old-time government mule-whacker is fast passing away in Texas, and those of them who were ambitious loved their mules and prided themselves on their close drives; and the cowboy loved his mount, and was as desirous of approbation and applause as a congressman at the present day.

In the spring of 1851 a mule train of forty six-mule teams was loaded with an army supplies and ordered to Phantom Hill. I went with it as carpenter, hunter, etc. Colonel Abercrombie was sent along to take command of the post. He had a nice ambulance to haul him and his nice little wife, and he called her the pet name of "Dickey." When we got to the west fork of the Trinity it was swollen from heavy rains. I went in and waded it to see if we could cross.

It was only about waist deep and we began to prepare to cross. Colonel Abercrombie asked me if I would carry "Dickey" over. He said she was afraid to go over in the ambulance as the current might capsize it. As I was already wet, I said, "Yes, with pleasure." Miss "Dickey," as I will call her, was a very small, neat little woman, weighing about 100 pounds, which was nothing for me to carry at that time, particularly when the load was in the shape and substance that it was. So I picked her up and set her on my shoulder and made across, and when I set her little feet on the south bank of West Trinity the temptation was so great that I had to give her a nice, little brotherly hug. She smiled and thanked me for bringing her safely across. I respectfully raised my hat and replied, "It is yours and the Colonel's to command; it is mine to obey."

Our train moved on to Phantom Hill, unloaded and returned to Fort Smith. As it passed Preston Major Wood, the quartermaster at that place, wanted me to stop with him, which I did. In the fall he received orders to abandon the quartermaster's department at Preston and go to Austin and take charge at that place. I went with him in charge of his wagon train. After we got to Austin he placed me under Major Albert Sidney Johnston, who was then paymaster in the United States army, with headquarters at Austin. He paid off the troops at Fort Crogan, Phantom Hill, Belknap, Graham and Fort Worth.

At that time there was not a house where Fort Worth now stands. The old post was occupied by one company of dragoons, commanded by Captain James Oaks. In 1852, or 1853, Lieutenant-Colonel R. E. Lee did command at Phantom Hill, although history says not. At that time the post was occupied by several companies of the Fifth Infantry.

A train of forty six-mule teams was loaded with government supplies for Phantom Hill, with orders to move Lieutenant Colonel R. E. Lee with five companies of the Fifth Infantry to Fort McIntosh, Laredo, on the Rio Grande.

I was with the train as carpenter from start to finish. The season was very bad, waters were high, and we were a long time on the road. We were two weeks getting across the Nueces at old Fort Ewell.

On this trip I was very much impressed with the soldierly bearing and Christian simplicity of Colonel Lee.

I was in government employ continuously from the spring of 1849 to December 20th, 1855, I might say on the frontier of Texas, in the various capacities of teamster, wagonmaster, carpenter, scout, dispatch bearer and, like David Copperfield of old, doer of odd jobs; in which time I have seen as many of the officers who did United States duty here on the frontier as any living man, I suppose.

## CAPT. W. J. MALTBY INTERVIEWED BY A REPORTER REPRESENTATIVE.

(Abilene Reporter, May 22, 1891.)

Capt. W. J. Maltby, one of the most prominent Texas farmers and horticulturists, favors the Reporter with the following interview. Capt. Maltby needs no introduction to the progressive farmers of this State; he needs no introduction to the horticulturists of the United States, with whom he has met in national convention at the annual meetings of the American Horticultural Society. He is a member in high standing of this organization, and is also a member of the Texas Horticultural Society, and is on important committees of both. The reporter asked:

"May I ask you what you think of the future of Abilene and the Abilene country?"

"I think that in the near future Abilene will be a city of 50,000 inhabitants."

"Why do you think so?"

"Because it has the three first great natural advantages to make it a city: (1) Health—a perfect absence from malaria. (2) Location —distance from other places of note. (3) Fertility of its soils and vastness of their extent. Every observing man that travels over the Abilene country will be convinced that there is not now, nor never can be, any local cause for sickness, which is the first consideration in any country. As to location, must say that it is the best located of any inland city in the State. It is directly in the geographical center of the State, and Texas, as a State, will be the wonder of the world and the center, like the center of man or beast, is the vital part. The name Abilene should be changed to Central City, which would add one million dollars to it and the country the first year.

"Abilene is destined to become one of the leading railroad centers of the State, the natural gaps in the mountains on direct lines to the seaboard south, and to Denver, Colorado, and Santa Fe north, the lines running their entire length through fertile agricultural, horticultural and the best of stock-raising countries, which will make them paying roads from the start, insures their building at an early date. As to the citizens and business men of Abilene, they are worthy to occupy the goodly country of their choice. For morals, hospitality, enterprise, 'git up and git' they may have equals, but no superiors; and let me make the assertion, without fear of contradiction, that for morals and orderly conduct, Abilene takes the lead.

"In case a flow of water is not reached in the artesian well what will Abilene do for a supply of water to support a city? That cuts no figure in the case whatever. Abilene has a never failing spring of pure water of sufficient volume, and with sufficient elevation, to put the water 100 feet above the city, for a city of any size or capacity."

"Then do you think that the Abilene country is an agricultural and horticultural country, and the place for the industrious, enterprising homeseeker and capitalist?"

"I do."

"Are you a practical farmer and fruit grower?"

"I am."

"How long have you lived in this country?"

"I am the pioneer or one of the pioneers. My advent into this country dates back to the location of Forts Belknap and Phantom Hill, in the year 1850."

"What has been your experience and observation in regards to rain fall sufficient to make general crops?"

"I have seen the country settle up from Red river to the Rio Grande on the thirty-second parallel, and the history of each county west as it settled up has been the same. Too dry for two or three years to make farming successful, but as more land was put into cultivation and the prairie fires were stopped that destroyed and stunted the growth of the forests and native trees, the rainfall increased each year, until there is an abundance and oft-times too much for successful farming."

"But the Abilene country has had serious drouths which have materially retarded its progress?"

"I admit that, but such a thing will never occur again, because our seasons are so long, and on any 100 acres of our tillable soil in the Abilene country, any intelligent, practical and well-to-do farmer can grow all the grain, grasses, fruit, flowers and vegetables that grow in the temperate zone. Under favorable seasons intelligence and perserverance, backed by long seasons and the best virgin soil of vast extent, will never record failure."

"How do you think our climate and fruit in the Abilene country will compare with California?"

"Very favorably, the difference in the climate is the way the thing is done. The Californians sell climate for from $100 to $500 per acre and throw in the land. The Abilene country sells land for from $5 to $25 per acre, and throws all the right they have to the climate in, and there isn't more than a nickel's difference in the climate, taken all through. The fruit of the future will vie with the fruit of California, with nearness to market in favor of the Abilene country."

"Have you lands for sale or are you interested in the sale of land?"

"No, I have no lands for sale nor am I interested in anyway wnatever with the sale of lands, but shall buy, as fast as my limited means will allow me, and keep as a heritage for my children."

## *HOMES FOR THE PEOPLE, WEALTH FOR THE STATE AND JUSTICE FOR THE HOWLERS.*

Editor Sentinel:

As you are in the middle of the road and desirous of giving justice to all men, politically and otherwise, for the advancement of our State and the betterment of its people, as you see it, I submit this article asking your comments and the comments of others on a subject that has engrossed my attention for many years, and, from my point of view, a question of no small importance to the State of Texas and its people. I wish to incite thought and get the people to commenting, for "in the multitude of counsel there is wisdom," saith the Scripture; again, "there is a time to all things," and again, "cast thy bread upon the water, and it shall be gathered up many days hence," etc. So I here make the bold assertion, without the fear of successful contradiction that the State of Texas has a rich gold mine in the proper enactment of a scalp law—a mine that will "pan out" more gold and more happiness to its people than any gold mine in California.

The wealth of a State consists in its public improvements and in the homes and happiness and prosperity of its citizens. With the proper enactment of a scalp law Texas can furnish homes to thousands of poor but deserving tenant farmers who never would be able to obtain a home under present conditions; and the waste places of West Texas can be made to rejoice and blossom as the rose, and the song of the hardy pioneer and his happy children to echo from Dan to Beersheba in praise of the State that utilized a curse and converted it into an untold blessing.

The prairie dogs of West Texas are worth as much to the State as the land, if utilized as they should and can be. If the State will put a bounty of 5 cents each on prairie dog scalps and make it sure and secure for the space of ten years, every section of agricultural land in West Texas will be dotted with homes, and the increase in taxable values will in twenty years treble what it now is which would be bread cast upon the waters, returning three-fold after many days, and many people made prosperous and happy.

Now, for the gold mine. If the State will put this 5-cent bounty on prairie dog scalps, and make it permanent and secure for the space of ten years, then the foundation is laid for the people of the State to realize 10 cents clear on each dog; that is, it would put that amount of money in circulation out of something that is worse than nothing, as is generally considered. We have boarded and lodged Mr. Prairie Dog for lo! these many years, and he can be made to pay handsomely for his entertainment. Estimating that there are fifty million prairie dogs in West Texas, and that ten cents on each one of them can be put into circulation, we see that it would add five million dollars to the circulation in West Texas, out of worse than nothing as viewed from an ordinary standpoint. But as all questions have two sides to them it may be that the dog was put in West Texas by a wise Providence to furnish the means whereby people could obtain homes. From my standpoint it would be easy to settle up West Texas by means of the prairie dog, but difficult unless we utilize this means. The way to realize the ten cents on each dog is for the State to properly fix the scalp law. When that is done and is generally known a grand and continued Oklahoma rush will be made for the school lands of West Texas. If properly set on foot there will be a general demand for their pelts and oil. Their pelts will command 5 cents apiece and each dog will render 5 cents worth of fine oil, which will put into circulation among the people $5,000,000 in the space of ten years, which amount will be used in the purchase of lands and the making of homes, resulting in a richer mine for Texas than any in California.

To go into the general details of this subject would make this article too long. My object is to incite thought and invite criticism, as the time for the destruction and utilization of the destructive animals of West Texas has probably come.

Prairie Doggie, thine for the right, homes for the people, and justice and progress for the howlers. W. J. MALTBY.

I see an article in the Sentinel from the old captain. It sounds somewhat funny. I wonder if the captain ever had any experience in getting the ropes on the worthless little doggie that he thinks there is so much money in. The hide may be all right, and the tallow too; the question is how to catch the dog in quantities that would pay. Will not the time and expense overrun the profits? I have managed to kill the dogs off twenty acres with poison and carbon and if ever I found a dead dog on top of the ground I do not remember it. And even if I could poison the dog and get him I would not like to pull the pelt from him. I think the Captain was letting his mind wander off in imagination and was thinking of the wonderful wealth that could be accumulated in case the doggie was as large as a mule and as fat as a bear in mast time. His idea that there was more money in that worthless dog than in the richest gold mine in California was purely imaginary and not real. I think a successful recipe how to kill the doggie would bring the dog catchers more money than the 5-cent tax and the hide and tallow put together. Just think of the tenant farmers out in West Texas catching dogs and selling hides and tallow and paying for the land that he caught the dogs off. Putting $5,000,000 in circulation would be worth wonders in West Texas. I will agree with the Captain that if the State will pay 5 cents for the scalp, and 10 cents can be had for the hide and oil, and they can be caught in large quantities so that the expense will not be so great, the $5,000,000 can be put in circulation. In multitude of counsel there is wisdom, and in killing a multitude of prairie dogs there is much labor and expense. I hope the Captain will go into the details of this wonderful scheme. There is a time for all things and there must be a time to kill prairie dogs, and I find it a difficult matter to kill them out of their dens. I wonder what Middle, South and East Texas would say to taxing them to kill the dogs for West Texas. I fail to see the point where exterminating the dogs would bring prosperity and happiness to its citizens. With proper enactment of a scalp law Texas can furnish homes to thousands of poor and deserving tenant farmers is another statement that needs to be explained, especially to as shortsighted a man as I am. The Captain slings a ready pen and gets off in fine style, but fails to make his points. There is not a tenant farmer who is able to go into the dog killing business, who is not able to take up a school claim and go to farming and make a good living, and kill the dogs off his own land without a scalp law. My guess is that I am into it now and there will not be a grease spot left of me when the Captain gets through with me. There is one point the Captain made. He said the editor of the Sentinel is in the middle of the road. C. A. CLEMMER.

## HOMES FOR THE PEOPLE AND WEALTH FOR THE STATE

(West Texas Sentinel, Abilene, Texas, March 12, 1893.)

Editor Sentinel:

Under the above heading, in your issue of February 17th, you published an article from me on the scalp law, in which I made some bold and unqualified assertions, and left all the gaps down and invited comments and criticisms, to which I took as a text or quoted three passages of Scripture, to-wit: (1st.) In the multitude of counsel there is much wisdom. (2nd) Bread cast upon the waters will return after many days. (3rd) A time to all things.

In the first place, I am proud to know that buncombe speeches and buncombe articles in newspapers don't go with men who claim to be in the middle of the road; that it takes "brass tack" arguments to win, and that if a thing is so why is it so. So I doff my hat in great respect to Bro. C. A. Clemmer for taking up the gauntlet that I threw down. For agitation is the life of all things. We must agitate and tickle the soil with plow and hoe and it will smile in corn and other useful and necessary products. So when the public mind is agitated on questions of importance it will smile in wisdom from a multitude of counsel. So Bro. C. can drive a tack here.

Bro. C. said that I made one point—that The Sentinel was in the middle of the road; so we here drive a brass tack. As to my experience in getting the ropes on the worthless little kuss of a prairie dog, let me say that I have made and eaten many savory pot-pies out of the little kuss long before he made his appearance in the Abilene country, and I here offer to bind myself to make one or tens of thousands of traps at 10 cents each that can be handled by any six-year-old boy or girl with perfect success, and be as durable as any other farm implement and not injure the scalp, hide or tallow. Those that are one-half or two-thirds grown are as good to eat as squirrels, the older ones, after being rendered, their meat can be fed to the pigs. So we will use the little fellow, lock, stock and barrel, and sing: Doggie, doggie, huah, huah, ah, huah. O, my little doggie, huah, huah, huah, hu or hey," and Bro. C. can drive a tack here.

Their pelts will make the best quality of kid gloves, and that kind of leather is very scarce all over the world. They will not render as much oil as a fat "b"ar" in mast time, but we will make up in quality what we lack in quantity, as it is proven to be the finest machine oil for all classes, even the sewing machine, and we are going to get 5 cents worth out of each "purp," and Bro. C. can drive a tack here.

Now, if there are fifty millions (which there are) of the worthless little kusses and four of their pelts will make a pair of first-class kid gloves, and each one will render on an average 5 cents worth of the very best of oil, and that they can be trapped, pelted and rendered by children too small to do hard labor, and that the inventive genius of the American people can and will supply the means for his (the doggy's) successful capture, without poison; and that by the proper enactment of a scalp law as a basis or foundation to build upon their pelts and oil will come into demand and will be current money at all the stores in West Texas, and the money will be drawn from other and manufacturing States and put in circulation in Texas; which will make in the aggregate a richer mine for Texas than any named mine in California. After the multitude of counsel if this proves to be wisdom, a tack can be driven here.

As to what Eastern and Southern Texas would say in regard to taxing them to pay for the scalps of the destructive animals of West

Texas, my reply is that whatever is to the great interest of any large portion of the State is to the interest of the whole State. In proof, under Governor Coke's administration a battalion of Rangers was voted for and organized by the vote of all Texas, and for the protection of West Texas against the Indians, which has proven, after a multitude of counsel, to have been great wisdom. For if only viewed from a financial standpoint, the increase of taxation that we have drawn from other States has much more than paid all the cost; which was bread cast upon the waters which was returned after many days, and many lives and much valuable property protected and the people made prosperous and happy. We will drive a tack here.

As it takes more space to answer a question than it does to ask it, and as space in The Sentinel is valuable, "A time to all things," and "homes for tenant farmers," by permission of The Sentinel, will appear later on. Some brass tacks left, and gun loaded with doggies and loaded for "b'ar." W. J. MALTBY.

*Reply.*

Putnam, Texas, February 27, 1893.

Editor Sentinel:

## CAPT. W. J. MALTBY'S LETTER ADRESSED TO THE BELLE PLAINE ALLIANCE, CALLAHAN COUNTY, TEXAS.

(From West Texas Sentinel, Abilene, Texas, March 8, 1893.)

Mr. D. Campbell, President Belle Plaine Alliance.

Dear Sir and Brother: Circumstances over which I have no control prevent my being present with you in person at your meeting on the third Saturday in February. I therefore address the meeting with my pen, through you, on matters pertaining to the "good of the order."

Brethren and Sisters—Although I cannot be with you in person to-day, let this suffice as proof that my spirit is with you in your noble work of trying to better the condition of yourselves, your families and your fellow men morally, socially and financially. And when you take a retrospective survey of your work you ought to feel encouraged, for the Bible plainly says that a tree is known by its fruit, and "by their fruits shall ye know them."

The fruits that you have cultivated are morals, temperance, Christianity, brotherly love, justice and general reformation, advancements in agriculture, horticulture, the beautifying of homes and the happiness of their inmates and the betterment of your fellow citizens. The cultivation of such fruits as these cannot bring the blush of shame to the cheek of any man or woman inside the bounds of civilization or within God's moral vineyard. Then you must receive the applaudit, "Well done, thou good and faithful servants." If you are conscious of having done your duty and that your labors have brought forth good fruit, you are enjoined in the Bible that as you have put your hand to the plow you must not turn or look back, but with the eye of faith fixed steadily forward, onward and upward (in the middle of the road, so to speak), neither turning to the right nor the left, but with full confidence in God's promise to the righteous that he should "never be forsaken nor his seed be found begging bread," asking justice for yourselves and granting the same to all others, demanding equal rights to all and special privileges to none, neither morally, socially or politically, so far as the government is concerned —advancements all along the line in the condition and intellectual training of the producing classes. Whenever and whatever the producing classes are intelligent, prosperous and happy all other occupations flourish. Then the legitimate conclusion must be that the producer is the leaven that leaveneth the whole lump; and anything that legislative or other influences can bring to bear to better its condition morally, socially, financially and politically betters his home, betters his neighborhood, betters his county, betters his State and betters his general government. The true fundamental principles of democratic government begin in a log cabin or home, and whatever will mete out equal justice and advancement to each member of that family will mete out the same to the neighborhood, county, State and general government.

The sword of Washington and the pen of Jefferson gave to us the greatest country and the grandest constitution under the sun. The pen of Jefferson wrote the words that made tyrants and crowned heads tremble, and that will live until time shall be no more—the words, "All men are born free and equal." Then, as I see it, the fruits of the alliance and the objects sought are equal protection to all classes of men, special privileges to none; equal representation, equal taxation, equal opportunities to beautify the earth and make it a fit temporary abode for man, and a proper footstool for the Author of man's existence. Thomas Jefferson was the greatest horticulturist of the age in which he lived. He planted the tree of democracy, and planted its roots in good, virgin soil, and its roots went downward and its trunk went upward and its branches spread outward until it gave shade and protection to the American people. And he left the people to dress and keep it, and he solemnly warned them that "eternal vigilance is the price of liberty," and told them that whenever any of the branches became decayed and failed to bear the fruit for which it was planted they were to be lopped off and new branches permitted to grow out in their stead and bear the required fruit, and the name of the fruit was "The greatest good to the greatest number—forever." To which every true alliance man will respond "Amen! God grant, and so mote it be."

Now, my friends, I wish to relate a little anecdote on an old darky and make an application to show the vanity of mankind had they the audacity to express themselves as the old darky did. Just after the war, when the darkies thought the bottom rail had gotten on top, an old darky down in Eastern Texas ran for the legislature and in his speeches he always quoted the constitution thusly: "My fellow citizens—Old Mars Jefferson he say in de declarshun ob independence dat all men am born'd free an' equal, and he furdermore says dat if enybody hab de preferens gib it to de darky." Now, to illustrate: If it were left to the banker, he would say "Give it to the banker." The merchant would say, "Give it to the merchant." The lawyer woul say, "Give it to the lawyer." The doctor would say, "Give it to the doctor," and the meek and lowly man—the preacher—he too would say, "If any man has the preference give it to the preacher." And last but not least, my friends, old Hayseed, too, would exclaim with a rising voice, "Give it to the farmer." And, as I am a sort of a jack-leg farmer myself I hope my vanity may be pardoned, for I would reiterate the language of the old darky and say, "If enybody hab de preferens, gib it to de farmer." The farmer may have some excuse for his vanity. If we believe the Bible (and most of us do), we read in

Genesis that in the beginning, after all other animated things had been created, God said: "Behold, there is not a man to till the soil." And God took the dust of the earth and made man, and breathed into his nostrils the breath of life, and man became a living soul. And God named him Adam—the father of all living. And the Lord God planted a garden over eastward in Eden, over which he placed that man Adam, the father of all living, to cultivate the soil and to dress the garden and keep it. So Adam, Abraham, Isaac, Jacob, Noah and all the patriarchs of old were cultivators of the soil (or flock masters, which is nearly the same), and the Bible further tells us that a stream cannot rise higher than its fountain. Then, if we are descendants of Adam we cannot rise above him. He was a farmer, and received his occupation from God himself, as the leading occupation of the earth. Then all other occupations must be secondary to this. You have the highest authority that your calling is noble and pure. You are the men who make nations and armies and sustain them. You are men who have planted the banners of your country upon the highest pinnacles of fame, and have everywhere subdued foes and built happy homes in their stead. You are the men who have founded this government that was cemented by the pen and constitution of Jefferson, and perpetuated by the loyal devotion of Lincoln, and should its hour of supreme peril ever come your dauntless legion, with devoted patriotism, will protect it unto salvation. In chorus—as one man— "This republic of Washington and Lincoln must be respected by all the world, and its benign constitution must, can and shall be administered in the interest of all classes of its citizens alike, by the Eternal, so help us God!"

With love for all and malice toward none, I am thine for the right.

W. J. MALTBY.

## OLDEN TIME MEMORIES.

*Letters from a Man Who Lived in Fort Smith Nearly Sixty Years Ago.*

(Fort Smith, Ark., Elevator, September 29, 1905.)

W. J. Weaver has received a letter from Jeff Maltby, a Fort Smith boy, of whom the Dallas News recently published a sketch rerelating his history in Western Texas. Jeff has done rough riding and killed more wild Indians than Roosevelt, Buffalo Bill or Kit Carson. He enlisted in Fort Smith for the Mexican war in Allen Woods and Felch's company, fought through the campaign, and afterwards served as an escort for Paymaster Albert Sidney Johnston in his trips to the far western posts—Forts Concho, Worth, Belknap, Arbuckle and Phantom Hill. There were many bad Indians on the southwestern frontier then, who made frequent raids on the western Texas settlers, scalped them and carried off women and children prisoners. These tribes were the Kiowas, Comanches, etc. They were desperate fighters and splendid horsemen. The Tonkaways were cannibals, and when they killed an enemy roasted and ate his legs and arms. Jeff then served through the Civil War with the Confederates. After the Civil War he served for some time as captain of a company of rangers, in the employ of the State of Texas, to protect the frontier counties from Indians and outlaws. The letter is dated at Admiral, Texas, and is as follows:

W. J. Weaver, Fort Smith, Ark.

My Dear Old Friend: I was surprised and delighted to get your letter, and return thanks to God that we yet live and have been permitted to enjoy this privilege of correspondence. I am 76 years old and have had quite a checkered life, in some respects I have seemed to carry a charmed life.

You know my Mexican war history. After that I was for six years in government employ on the frontier of Texas in various capacities—carpenter, wagonmaster, scout, dispatch bearer, teamster, hunter, etc. Like David Copperfield of old, I was a doer of odd jobs for six years, after which, in 1856, I built a stage stand at Fort Clark to keep the men and mules that carried the United States mail from San Antonio to El Paso. In 1858 I rented out my premises to the mail company and went to Burnett, Texas, where I got married to one of God's noble helpmates to man and went to farming and stock raising, continuing scouting for Indians as the only way to save life and property. I followed this life up to the commencement of the Civil War, when I raised a company of men and joined the Seventeenth Texas Volunteer Infantry, C. S. A., served one year and was then sent back to the frontier of Texas and put in command of a company of men to guard the frontier against Indians, bushwhackers, deserters, etc. I held this position until the close of the war, and was courtmartialed for holding the position long after Lee's surrender. Since that time I have commanded several ranger companies, it is said with honor to the State and credit to myself, and I have never been hurt in any way.

My wife is 67 years old, and we have had eight fine children. We are living in what is said to be the most pleasant home in Callahan County, Texas, where we have planted with our own hands all manner of fruits and flowers, and where we rest under our own vine and fig tree, quietly waiting for the call from the land of the leal, where I hope and expect to sit down and smoke the pipe of peace with the Indians that I have assisted from this to their happy hunting grounds, and there, with all nations of this earth, fully recognize and acknowlege the universal Fatherhood of God and the Brotherhood of Man. Remember me kindly to all old-timers.

With best wishes for your longer life and happiness, I am, your old friend, W. J. MALTBY.

*FRUIT AND TRUCK GROWING IN WEST TEXAS.*

(West Texas Sentinel, Abilene, Texas, Feb. 12, 1902.)

Mr. President and Members of the Farmers' Institute of the Abilene Country:

I have been honored and requested by your honorable association to deliver an address or read a paper before you, and the subject assigned to me, "The Outlook for Gardening and Fruit Growing in the Abilene Country," is a subject of great magnitude and of vital importance to the growth, prosperity and greatness of my country. There is no country that can ever be truly a great country whose soils and climate fails to respond bountifully to the efforts of the tiller of soil when the proper propagation and cultivation is rightly applied.

These words, "rightly applied," is some of the big clods that we clodhoppers run up against in all new countries, which calls for farmers' institutes and experience meetings in good old campmeeting style, telling how the Lord had blessed their labors, etc.

These experience meetings, when properly appreciated and regularly attended, will soon make the barren and waste places blossom as the rose. "God made the tillers of the soil the beautifiers of the earth, His footstool," he was the last and crowning piece of creation and placed in the Garden of Eden to keep it and dress it.

Mr. President, my invitation to address this meeting on the Outlook for Fruit Growing and Gardening, carries with it right to make suggestions. The Abilene country now has two of the greatest auxilaries in the rapid development of agriculture and horticulture, which are the West Texas Fair and Farmers' Institute.

The West Texas Fair should be supported and encouraged by every business man and farmer in the country. and I would suggest that the directors of the Fair employ the right man and put him in the right place to encourage the farmers to get up exhibits of everything that grows in the county, and to visit every town and try to interest every business man to chip in and offer special premiums for all the different products of merit that can be got together and exhibited at the West Texas Fair. There will be no trouble to get up exhibits that will compare favorably with any country, if we can only get the special premiums offered. The race horse comes in for too great a share in proportion to agriculture and horticulture.

We know that the race horse is a drawing card, and the raising of fine stock should be encouraged to its fullest extent, commensurate with the products of the farm. The rains come and the winds blow and the race tracks are wiped out, but the farm and orchard are living and abiding monuments of their durability and sustaining qualities.

The Farmers' Institute, like experimental stations, should be kept up, honored and encouraged. The adage that like begets like, holds good in agriculture as in anything else, for when one farmer finds out what variety of seeds to plant and what variety of fruit trees to plant and what nursery to get his trees from, then his neighbors should follow his example, and if so his neighbor is benefited.

And now, my brothers of the Farmers' Institute, the Bible tells us that he that don't provide for his own household has denied the faith, etc. We have within our household as noble, intelligent, honorable and scientific a lot of nurserymen as the world can produce; such as E. W. Kirkpatrick, T. V. Munson, John S. Kerr, F. T. Ramsey and others, who have spent years and years propagating and experimenting to get the best fruit of all varieties best adapted to our climate and soils. They can tell you how to select the location, how to plant, how to prune, how to cultivate, and when your trees come to bearing, you have got just what they told you you would have.

I believe I am considered the pioneer fruit grower in the Abilene country, and my sad experience with fruit tree agents has so completely cut my eye teeth that if I were going to plant one or ten thousand trees, I would order them from E. W. Kirkpatrick or T. V. Munson and pay them their price, before I would take the same number of trees from any nursery outside of the State as a gift. Tree planting should interest every business man and every householder in the country, and I bespeak a careful interest in what your gifted and experienced townsman, the Hon. Henry Sayles, has to say. His words should be treasured as "apples of gold in goblets of silver," and if so, they will be like grain that fell on good soil and will bring forth a hundred fold. The planting of trees and the making of lovely and happy homes should be man's greatest object here on earth. He should, if he is able to do so, plant everything that is pleasing to the eye, fragrant to the smell and delicious to the palate. This is the subject that seems to give us a stepping stone to that land that is fairer than this, where we hope to pluck ambrosial fruit from trees immortal grown.

Mr. President, and gentlemen of the Institute, the subject that has been assigned to me is like space, it has no end and cannot be entered into in one short address, therefore I give way to some other gentleman that can interest you more intelligently and profitably than I have.

In conclusion let me say that agriculture and horticulture have more civilizing and Christianizing influences surrounding them than any other occupation under the sun. Stock raising is the occupation of the barbarous and semi-barbarous nations of the earth. Manufacturers are the breeders of anarchism, alcoholism, poverty and crime. You may admire the stockman with his broad acres and his cattle grazing upon a thousand hills—you may admire the factory with its thousands of busy spindles, but what civilizing influences do they possess? But agriculture and horticulture are the handmaidens of religion, law and order everywhere, for who can stand beside the tree laden with its golden fruit, or the vine with its purple clusters, or the rose in its superlative loveliness, without worshipping the God that gave these gifts to man.

Admiral, Texas.

*SPEECH MADE BY CAPT. W. J. MALTBY TO THE CITIZENS OF HIS NATIVE COUNTY, SANGOMAN, AT THE CENTRAL ILLINOIS STATE FAIR, VIRGINIA, ILL., AUG. 6, 1891, AS TAKEN BY THE SHORT HAND REPORTER AND GIVEN TO US.*

Ladies and gentlemen and fellow countrymen of my nativity—We read away back in sacred history, where Moses sent out a horticultural deputation to view, the land and to bring back samples of the fruits, so that the children of Israel could judge whether it was goodly land to immigrate to. The difference between that first horticultural deputation, and this Texas on wheels, of which I am a delegate is this: Moses sent out his deputation, whereas the people of the great State of Texas have sent their deputation to you with magnificent cars laden with the grand products of the Lone Star State, and samples of her citizens. Governor Hubbard represents the acme of society, oratory and statesmanship, while I, your humble servant, represent the wild and wooly cowboy of the west, or the rare old plainsman of fiction, that went around with a sythe blade for a toothpick and a pistol eight or nine feet long, loaded with a ball weighing anywhere between twenty-five and seventy-five pounds, with spurs and other accoutrements to match. Such, my friends, are the pictures drawn of Western Texas cow men, but, like all the pictures of Texas, they are overdrawn, all but the facts.

Now, my friends, one of the facts connected with the exhibit is this: That I have no land for sale, and that I am not interested in any way, with any man or firm that has lands for sale, is one reason that the people of Texas wanted me to come, and the other reason is my long residence in the State of Texas.

Having seen the country settle up through its center from the Red river to the Rio Grande, and the history of each county has been the same merged from stock raising to farming, and each farm has been capable of producing all the cereals, all the varieties of fruits, vines and vegetables; and let me say to you that after having traveled over most of the States and Territories, that I believe Texas to be the best field for the investment of capital, the best for the homeseeker, the man with the hoe; to obtain cheap and fertile lands. Our car arrived on your grounds yesterday, after a direct run from Denison, Texas. I was very tired and had a very refreshing sleep last night, and woke up this morning perfectly refreshed, and my mind wandered back all over my past life; how I had been a volunteer in the Mexican war of '46 and '47, and how I had been in the employment of the United States on the frontier as carpenter, teamster, scout, dispatch bearer, etc. For seven years, from Red River to the Rio Grande, outside of the settlements, but was the home of the blood-thirsty, cruel savage Indian, that murdered in cold blood defenseless women and children, whenever the opportunity offered. When the war between the States was fully inaugurated, I espoused the cause of the South, for it was my home, and went through the war. After the war I followed the avocation of cowboy and Texas ranger until peace spread her white wings over the frontier of Texas. I then beat my sword into a pruning hook and my pistol into a plow share, and have since that time turned my attention to the peaceful pursuits of agriculture and horticulture, in what is now known as the Abilene country of Texas. Go and inspect Texas on wheels and you will say: "Peace hath her victories, as well as war."

And now, my countrymen, after going through what I have narrated to you, my heart melts in thankfulness to the giver of all good, that after a lapse of sixty years, I have been permitted to open my eyes in the land where they first saw the light, or the land of my birthplace. Has my life been spared to bring to you the glad tidings of the modern star of Bethlehem—the Lone Star of Texas? These productions of the earth are strictly specimens of the fertility of Texas soils. They were not sent to you by the people of Texas, asking you to sell out happy and comfortable homes, unless you are perfectly satisfied that you can better the condition of yourself and family. We come to let you know that such a country as Texas does exist, that its people are law-abiding and moral, that they welcome you to come, that your religion or politics will not debar you from the best society. But come to make two blades of grass grow where only one grew before, not expecting to gather grapes of thorns or figs of thistles, but expecting each tree and vine will bring forth fruit after its own kind, when properly cared for and planted. To all such we say: Come; we pledge to you a country where you can sit down under your own vine and fig tree, where none can or dare to molest.

---

Texas rolled into Chicago Sunday night on wheels. It came in three large red railroad coaches, which were hauled along the Atchison, Topeka and Santa Fe tracks to Sixteenth street. There the three cars stood all day yesterday, blinding the vision of people that flashed by in passenger trains. Some time to-day the cars will be dragged further into the city and by to-night may be resting on the lake front if Stuyvesant Fish makes no objection. Yesterday old Capt. W. J. Maltby, who went into the Rio Grande country in 1850, and for a long while commanded a troop of the State rangers along that ragged and reckless frontier, wrapped his arm around an ear of corn in one of the cars, and said, "Yes suh, we raise something in Texas now besides h—l." Captain Maltby, after tumbling about with six-shooters on his hips for a quarter of a century, has now settled down on one of the farms he owns in the Abilene country, and is one of the famous and successful horticulturists and agriculturists in the big, sprawling State. The Capt'n has charge of the coaches of the Texas exhibit. The display is made by the Texas Real Estate Association and will be rolled around the country for a whole year. Col. W. B. Slosson, director and manager of the association, is in charge, and there are living with him on the coaches: Emigrant Agent T. A. Wilkinson, of the Rio Grande Railway; ex-Governor R. B. Hubbard, who lectures on the exhibit; W. M. Fagle, the press agent, and W. R. Roberts, nephew and private secretary of the governor and advertising distributer. Captain Maltby is likewise on the red train and also all over it.

*Something of Everything.*

There is everything in those cars. There are products from the Texas plains and the Texas penitentiaries; from the Texas fields and the Texas factories. The products are of this year's growth, and contain specimens of corn, cotton, wheat, oats, rye, barley, walnut, white and red oak, bois d'arc, whatever that is, cedar, gum, dogwood, ash, holly, persimmon, plum, pine, maple, water-live-oak, white hickory and slippery elm wood. Then there are grey granite, sandstone and limestone, hydraulic limestone, fire clay, lignite, vegetable marl, red and yellow ochre, brown laminate, brown hematite, coal, brick and vitrified or paving brick, iron ore from 40 to 67, mill iron, silver gray, mottled and car wheels. There are also articles representing the manufacture of leather and blankets, all the grades of cotton goods, flour, packing and canning house products. And right beside these ranged along through the cars are apples, peaches, pears, plums, grapes, quinces, beans, tomatoes, okra, onions, peppers, bananas, oranges, lemons, cucumbers and muskmelons. Captain Maltby has a muskmelon raised on his farm, which is three feet long and he doesn't brag on it either. He has it sealed in a jar now. It was growing when he started but it grew so fast and furiously that the people on the car couldn't breathe. The Cap'n also had some growing grapes when the train left Galveston three weeks ago, but in coming out of Lincoln, Ill., the other day, the colonel left the door open, the vines ran out, wrapped themselves about the telegraph wires, and during the electric shock which the inhabitants of the car received, the vines grew so rapidly that they dragged the train back into Springfield.

"These hyah yeahs of cawn," said Captain Maltby yesterday, slapping a big fat jar in one of the cars, "were raised by me down on my fahm in the Abilene country this spring. The first plat of six acres was planted March 15th, the second plat of six acres was planted April 1st; the third of six acres, April 15th; the fourth of six acres, May 1st and the fifth of four acres, May 15th. Theah's nine varieties of large field corn in that jah suh, and I consider it the finest exhibit of cawn evah made. I didn't raise it for an exhibit, but just to keep up a succession of roastin' yeahs. The ground was sod land, and wasn't cross-broke neitha, suh. It never was plowed but twice, and then with an ordinary cultivator. Now this hyah yeah of cawn, suh," continued the captain, taking down a jar with a roasting ear in it that looked like a squash, "is the largest yeah of cawn in the world. I raised that myself, suh, and originated it. That sort of cawn in Texas is known as the Maltby cawn or the Abilene country nubbin. This yeah has thirty perfect rows on it and the grains are more than three quarters of an inch long. That's only second yeah cawn, suh, and ordinary cawn only has about eighteen rows to the yeah. Then these are nubbins." The captain plays with kernels of corn that might make a set of false teeth for a horse. These are just a few features of the exhibit with which these men are inviting the people from the northwest to Texas.

*New Ideas of Texas.*

A stuffed tarpon, the largest game fish in the world, stares at their visitors from the door. This one is five feet eight inches long and weighs 110 pounds. This, too, is the largest tarpon ever caught that anybody knows of. It was hooked at Aransas Pass near Rockport. Then there is a pretty table of inlaid woods, exquisite in its workmanship, and contains twenty-nine native Texas woods. It was made by a convict in the penitentiary, and contains 178,889 pieces of wood.

The vividly painted cars are strung with mottos. Some of them say:

Fifty dollar fine and imprisonment for carrying concealed weapons in Texas.

One sheep ranch in Texas larger than the State of Rhode Island.

No card playing in Texas.

Taxes in Texas 20 cents on the $100.

If reciprocity has thousands for Massachusetts it has millions for Texas.

Out west is gone. Come to Texas.

Texas laws are better inforced than any other State.

The cars are covered with Texas scenes painted in oil. They will remain here eight days. Captain Maltby said there wasn't much liquor drank in Texas any more.—Chicago Herald.

The following letter complimentary to Capt. W. J. Maltby was received Friday:

Petersburg, Ill., Aug. 11, 1891.

Messrs. H. Henderson and F. Bompart.

My Dear Sirs: I wish to say in behalf of the "Texas Car Exhibit" (to which you and others have been and are still warm contributors) that the accession of my friend and old comrade, Capt. W. J. Maltby, of Callahan County, to our corps, was a most fortunate circumstance for all Texas. He is an old Texan and veteran; a soldier of the Mexican war and a gallant ranger and captain of one of our best companies during my administration as governor from 1876 to 1879, and since then, known throughout Texas as one of the most successful farmers and horticulturists in the famous Abilene country of Western Texas. All these antecedents and qualifications make his official connection with these exhibits of "Texas on Wheels" a very winning card. The exhibit so far has been warmly welcomed and has excited great inquiry about our whole State. It will bear good fruit. I am glad of the opportunity of thanking the Abilene friends of the exhibit for sending us Captain Maltby. Yours truly,

RICHARD B. HUBBARD.

Captain W. J. Maltby, of Abilene, an ex-captain of the State rangers, is with us, and is doing valiant service in the cause of Texas. He never fails to draw a crowd around him when recounting his early experiences in Texas, as contrasted with the present. The fact that he is a "sucker" gives him authority to speak by the book, and he is listened to with attention. He was born in Sangamon County, in this State, and to-day he is resting by the smiling waters of the Sangamon river, the first his eyes ever had sight of.

## THEY WERE COMANCHES AND KIOWAS.

Admiral, Texas, Jan. 1, 1902.
Col. I. R. Hitt, Colorado City, Texas.
Dear Sir: As per your request, I herewith give you a brief recital of my acquaintance and transactions with the Indians. Since the year 1836 to the year of 1876, in my early life, my lines were cast in close proximity to the five civilized tribes and almost daily from 1836 to 1846 was among them, until I was perfectly familiar with them. In the year of 1849, I was employed by the acting quartermaster of the United States army at Fort Smith, Ark., in locating and hauling supplies to the different government posts, located in the Indian Nation and Texas, and was in such employ continuously for several years and while in such employment, I became acquainted with the friendly or the partly friendly tribes, to-wit: Caddos, Wacoes, Tonqueays, Lipans, Delawares, etc.

In the year of 1852 or 1853 a man by the name of Stell or Snell' made a treaty with the Comanches and Kiowas and set up a trading

post on the Clear Fork of the Brazos river half way between the
posts of Belknap and Phantom Hill, about forty miles from either
post. Shortly after Stell or Snell had established his trading post
and had got the aforesaid Indians to the number of 1000 to 2000
to come in, I visited the camp or trading post in company with
Maj. Albert Sidney Johnston, who was then paymaster in the
United States army and paid off the troops at the following posts,
to-wit: Fort Crogan in Hamilton valley, Burnett County; Phantom
Hill, Fort Belknap, Fort Graham and Fort Worth. Major Johnston remained in or at Snell's or Stell's trading post one day and night
and I studied the Indians very close as they were markedly different
in many respects to any Indians I had ever seen. They did not molest
us in any way but let us leave them in peace, but had they known
the treasure in gold and silver that Major Johnston had with him
this letter never would have been written; in proof, some short
time after they killed Mr. Agent, looted his camp and went back
to their former place and station. In 1855, Major Rough of the
United States Rifle Corps was sent out to guard the road from Fort
Clark to El Paso. I was sent with him. We had a fight with the
Muscalaries Apaches near Eagle Springs, and killed ten of them
and piled them up in one pile, and there was a marked difference
between them and the Indians that I saw at Snell's or Stell's trading post in 1856. I quit the United States service and built a stage
stand to keep the men and mules of the Overland Mail that ran
from San Antonio to El Paso. My stand was at Fort Clark. One
night the Indians came in and stole all the mail, mules and all
the horses but one, and that one was mine, and a good one, which
was soon saddled and mounted and the news carried to the commanding officer at Fort Clark. He ordered a scout at once and we

took the trail north, pressed it hard for thirty or thirty--five miles, overtook them, had a fight with them, killed two of them, one of them being dressed in my clothes that he had stolen out of the washtub at Fort Clark. The guide or trailer on this occasion was an old Mexican that the Comanches had stolen when he was a boy, and they had made a slave of him for many years. He scalped the dead Indians; he said they were Comanches and he wanted to get even with them for their many cruelties while he was their prisoner. They had the marks and peculiarities of the Indians that I saw at Stell's or Snell's trading post. In the year of 1857 I got *married* and settled in Burnett County and went to stock raising, and from that time on to 1876 was more or less in pursuit of Indians and in that number of years I necessarily saw some dead ones and live ones. and I pronounce all that I saw the same Indians that Stell or Snell had made the treaty with, and he said they were Comanches and Kiowas. In the spring of 1874 the State of Texas raised and equipped a battalion of State rangers. I raised and commanded one of the companies. My post of duty was over the counties of Brown, Coleman, Callahan, Runnels, Taylor, Tom Green, etc., and in the first six months of my service I had six separate engagements with the same tribes of Indians that I saw in or at Stell's or Snell's trading post.

Ask any old settler that you come in contact with if he had ever seen or heard of the Big Foot Indian that made the big tracks for many years over the counties of Burnett, Lampasas, Llano, Mason, San Saba, Coleman, Brown, etc. I myself, as one of a party have run or trailed him many times before the Civil War, many times during the Civil War, and on and on till the summer of 1874, when with my ranger company we met him and his band in Runnels County and the ranger charge was made in which the noted Big Foot

Indian fell and an old war scarred veteran of sixty or sixty-five years was mortally wounded, and fell into our hands. I speak the Mexican language and I had a Mexican in my company that spoke good English. The old wounded Indian spoke good Mexican and he seemed to be willing and anxious to talk. My men stood around while myself and Mexican Joe questioned him.

He said that he was a Comanche and his name was Jape or Japee, that Big Foot, the dead brave was a Kiowa chief, and that they had left Fort Sill four or five days before. He said that he or they had raided the settlements for many years, and that the many scars on his person were made by white men in the settlements. He said he helped to kill Wafford Johnson and family on Dog Branch, Burnett County, the Blalock or Whitlock family near Llano County, the Todd family in Mason County, and last, Bill Williams' family in Brown County, in 1874.

He said that they had carried one of Bill Williams' girls away off and hung her to a tree, which proved to be as he stated.

The way we put the questions to him in regards the killing of the different families and his answers led us all to believe at the time that he helped to do it all, as he could give the direction, the distance, the locations and the length of time, number killed, etc. He answered every question as readily as he could, but one, and that was the name of his Big Foot Chief. He said that he was a Kiowa chief but his name he would not tell.

We killed Indians of the same tribes while in this service at different times and they all had nice red blankets branded U. S.

Truly yours,            W. J. MALTBY.